What people are saying about …

Parenting Beyond Your Capacity

"As parents to six kids, nothing is more important to Amy and me than passing on our faith to the next generation of Groeschels. Reggie and Carey offer simple, solid steps to make that goal a reality for parents from any background."

Craig Groeschel, founding and
senior pastor of LifeChurch.tv

"As one of the founders of North Point Community Church and a proven innovator in family ministry, Reggie Joiner is in a terrific position to offer insight into how churches and families can align their strategy for the benefit of preschoolers, children, and teenagers."

John C. Maxwell, best-selling author of
The 21 Irrefutable Laws of Leadership

"If you are a parent and desire a close relationship with your children, this book is a must-read. Parenting is tough, and my life is so busy that I sometimes feel overwhelmed by parenting; sometimes I get so out of balance that I get discouraged. But this book will motivate you. This book will encourage you. If you want to stay focused on what really matters and move your relationship with your children in the right direction, this is the book for you."

Joel Manby, CEO of Herschend Family
Entertainment and father of four girls

"I love Reggie and Carey. And by the time you are a dozen or more pages into this book, you are going to love 'em too! In *Parenting Beyond Your Capacity,* they provide us with a practical and revolutionary approach to the responsibility most of us find daunting—parenting. At the heart of this book are *five family values* that I'm convinced will equip you to be successful throughout your child's development."

Andy Stanley, senior pastor of North Point Community Church

REGGIE JOINER
CAREY NIEUWHOF

PARENTING BEYOND YOUR CAPACITY

CONNECT YOUR FAMILY
TO A WIDER COMMUNITY

David C Cook®

transforming lives together

PARENTING BEYOND YOUR CAPACITY
Published by David C. Cook
4050 Lee Vance View
Colorado Springs, CO 80918 U.S.A.

David C. Cook Distribution Canada
55 Woodslee Avenue, Paris, Ontario, Canada N3L 3E5

David C. Cook U.K., Kingsway Communications
Eastbourne, East Sussex BN23 6NT, England

David C. Cook and the graphic circle C logo
are registered trademarks of Cook Communications Ministries.

All Scripture quotations, unless otherwise noted, are taken from the *Holy
Bible, New International Version®. NIV®.* Copyright © 1973, 1978, 1984 by
International Bible Society. Used by permission of Zondervan. All rights
reserved. Scripture quotations marked NLT are taken from the New Living
Translation of the Holy Bible. New Living Translation copyright © 1996, 2004
by Tyndale Charitable Trust. Used by permission of Tyndale House Publishers.

LCCN 2010923654
ISBN 978-1-4347-6481-2
eISBN 978-1-4347-0214-2

© 2010 Reggie Joiner and Carey Nieuwhof
Published in association with the literary agency of
D.C. Jacobson & Associates, LLC, an author management company
www.dcjacobson.com

The David C. Cook Team:
Don Pape, Caitlyn York, Amy Kiechlin, Sarah Schultz, Karen Athen
The reThink Team:
Sarah Anderson, Kristen Ivy, Mike Jeffries, Cara
Martens, Beth Nelson, and Karen Wilson.
Cover design: Studio Gearbox

Printed in the United States of America
First Edition 2010

3 4 5 6 7 8 9 10

061110

FROM REGGIE JOINER:

My wife, Debbie:

the only one in my family, or on the planet,

who has chosen to live with me for the rest of my life.

And to my children—Reggie Paul, Hannah, Sarah, and Rebekah;

they have all worked hard and patiently to raise a father.

FROM CAREY NIEUWHOF:

To my wife, Toni,

There is treasure in you no one will ever be able to exhaust.

Thank you for saying yes.

And to my sons, Jordan and Sam—

I could not be more pleased with who you are becoming.

Contents

Acknowledgments

Carey would like to thank:

My parents, Marten and Marja. Your prayers, faithful example, and relentless refusal to give up on me carry weight far beyond what you realize.

My family: Toni, Jordan, and Sam; my three sisters, Melissa, Wendy, and Jennifer; their families; and Toni's family. Thank you for loving me for who I am.

The incredible staff, elders, and people of Connexus Community Church. You are living what so many only talk about. I am so thankful I get to do this with you!

North Point Community Church and its strategic partners. Your leadership, humility, and kindness continue to encourage and challenge me.

Reggie and Debbie Joiner and the staff and board of reThink. I love a place that not only values family ministry but has become family. Thank you for graciously adopting me into a household filled with love, vision, and hope.

Reggie would like to thank:

Those on the reThink staff, who are advocates for these principles every day. Your daily efforts help thousands of churches make the family-church partnership a priority.

The Family Ministry staff at North Point Community Church, who helped form these principles in everyday practice. When we started North Point, we knew that families would be central to the way we built the church because they were already central to our own lives. That's the true Orange Factor.

Joel Manby and the reThink Board of Directors for believing in this vision. Don Jacobson for seeing the reach of this project. Lanny Donoho for standing beside me (literally) for more than a decade.

My parents, Rufus and Dee. They have believed in God and me as long as I can remember. My brother, Jimmy, who still believes in God, even though I have been in ministry most of his life. My mother-in-law, Betty Dean, who raised my wife to love God, our kids, and me.

The reThink editing team, for wrestling with the words and concepts in this book (and for all the times they stayed awake with me).

Together, we'd like to thank:

Orange Leaders everywhere in Canada, the United States, and beyond, who champion this cause by investing in the lives of kids, teenagers, and families. Your stories, friendship, and encouragement at conferences, at events, and online always remind us of a much bigger story God is writing.

All those parents and leaders who read early drafts of the book, for their detailed and very helpful critiques and encouragements.

Foreword

I read an article the other day about a wildly successful college football coach, and in the article he was talking about the cost of success. At one point he conceded, "I don't really know my children."

After I read this, I stopped and thought, *How sad.* The world had this guy on a pedestal, yet he had failed miserably at the most important assignment he was given during his time on earth. More importantly, the ramifications of his failure will probably be felt for decades to come.

Being a good parent is hard, and in the short term there is not a whole lot of glory attached to it. You can't coast through it. It is intentional. Anybody can have a child; being a good parent takes work and prayer.

But if anything is worth the effort, it's your children. Many people, like the football coach, get their priorities wrong. They devote too much time and effort to things that don't really matter.

A hundred years from now, your great-grandchildren probably won't even know your name. No one will care about what awards you won or how much money you made. The only thing that will matter is what kind of children you left behind and their influence on subsequent generations.

Many parents make the mistake of thinking that being "good" means giving children whatever they want, ignoring the costs either financially or emotionally. That isn't how the real world works, and to send them out into it unprepared is irresponsible.

Children need parents, not another "friend," though friendship is one of the end results of a job done right.

Children need a foundation of faith to sustain them when they reach the end of their abilities, strength, or control. (Ever been there yourself?)

Children need to fail. Not at the big things, but at the little ones. If you've never failed, you haven't tested the boundaries of your capabilities.

I can promise that even for the most intentional parents, there will be nights when all you can do is fold your hands and cry, "God, help me!" I imagine God hears that and thinks, "I thought you'd never ask!"

You will make plenty of mistakes, and that's okay. Mistakes are often opportunities to show your children not only your fragile humanity but also the way you respond to failure.

On the bright side, there are also days that you get a glimpse of the fruits of your labor. A few years back on Father's Day morning, I found a letter my fifteen-year-old daughter had taped to my bathroom mirror. It listed many things I thought were unnoticed

as examples of things that she loved and appreciated about me. The
letter concluded with this paragraph:

> You and Mom have raised us in the best Christian
> home possible and show us your belief, devotion,
> and obedience to God every day through your
> actions and decisions. I never doubt your morals or
> your motivations.

I know that's what the note says—because it's still there, and I
read it almost every day.

Like me, Reggie Joiner has worked at being a parent. I have
spent hours discussing the subject with him. It is one of his deepest
passions.

The very fact that you picked up this book and are reading it
shows that being a good parent is the cry of your heart as well.

Within these pages, Reggie Joiner and Carey Nieuwhof have laid
out a foundation of proven principles:

- the importance of faith and community,
- the power of relationship, and, most importantly,
- a message of encouragement that our success as parents
  is God's desire, and He has provided all we need for the
  task.

Reggie is an innovative and godly man and a natural-born communicator. When he talks, I listen. And when he writes, I want to
read it.

There is wisdom within these pages, and as I always joke to Reggie, "Wisdom equals knowledge plus scars."

He laughs and says, "I couldn't agree more."

Fight the good fight. It is so worth it.

God bless,

Jeff Foxworthy

Introduction

When Carey and I first started talking about writing a book on parenting, it wasn't because we believed we were parenting experts. We are simply dads who constantly try to remind each other about the important stuff related to our families. We both openly admit that we are

- somewhat dysfunctional,
- a little insecure,
- more stressed than we should be.

Oh, and there is one other fact that we will occasionally hide from strangers we meet. *We are both pastors.*

That means we have spent most of our adult lives working in churches to help people grow in their relationships with God.

We don't really consider ourselves to be experts on God or relationships. But we are both committed to a lifelong pursuit of figuring out how to love God and our families better, and to help other people do the same.

The ages of our children add up to nearly 120 years. That means we have collectively parented for over 43,500 days. So we have had a lot of time to experiment on our children. We have made a host of mistakes, but we have also had quite a few accidental discoveries that led to powerful and positive memories. Now that all of our children have turned out practically perfect, we are both comfortable writing a book about our parenting skills. (Not really … just checking to see if you were actually reading.) Let us rephrase: Now that we have realized there is something more important than getting your kids to "turn out right," we are compelled to write a book about what we are learning.

When I (Carey) met Reggie Joiner several years ago, he was the executive director of family ministry at North Point Community Church in Alpharetta, Georgia. He was one of the founding pastors who started the church with Andy Stanley in 1995. They had just written a book called *The Seven Practices of Effective Ministry*, and I invited Reggie to speak to a group of Canadian leaders about strategy. During one of the messages, he spoke on the need for the church to partner more effectively with the family. It radically changed the way I looked at my family and the families in my church. Since that day, the two of us have had countless conversations as we attempt to navigate through a variety of parenting stages.

Carey has become one of my (Reggie's) best friends over the past several years. As I've watched him work as a senior pastor, I have been inspired by the way he has built a remarkable church that makes families a priority. Carey is a unique leader. He first graduated from law school, then decided to go to seminary. He is a gifted communicator who has an authentic passion for the people in his community. After several years of leading a growing church outside Toronto, he started a new church called Connexus. Since 2005, Carey has helped our team communicate an Orange message to church leaders and parents locally and globally.

In this book, you'll hear about the color orange again and again. We use orange to symbolize the partnership we believe can exist between parents and the church. When you combine the *light* from a faith community (yellow) with the *heart* of a caring family (red), you exponentially expand your potential to make a difference in the life of a child. These two combined influences will make a greater impact than either influence alone.

One of the reasons we're writing this book is to let you know that you don't have to parent alone. Don't misunderstand. No one has more potential to impact your child or teenager than you. But one of the greatest ways you can impact the life of your child is to become intentional about partnering with others who can also have influence with your child. If you try to parent alone, you will just become increasingly aware of your built-in flaws and risk becoming discouraged and disillusioned with parenthood.

No matter how great our parenting skills, we all have limited capacity to accomplish this impossible responsibility. Society offers promises of a better picture that most of us can't achieve on our own. In fact, the high expectations make us more aware of just how far we have to go. That's why this isn't a self-help book. It's a get-help book. It's about how you can increase your parenting capacity by connecting with available resources, some of which you know about and some of which you might not.

Your weaknesses as a parent can work in your favor. They should remind you to pursue other influences for your family. Face this truth about parenting: Every parent has a different set of limitations. As you read these pages we hope you will learn to look beyond your limitations and embrace a set of principles that will help you influence your children beyond your own capacity.

The concepts we are going to discuss should be viewed as more of a compass than a road map. The last thing we want to do is create a new impossible standard, more parenting initiatives, and more tasks for you to do. Instead, we hope to establish a kind of framework to help you remember what's important.

Throughout the book we will refer to some of the ancient insights that Moses shared with the Hebrew people in order to influence their children. We will also offer personal stories to help illustrate Moses' thoughts and how we have seen them play out in our own lives.

Chapters three through seven explain five family values that can guide your approach to parenting. At the end of each of these chapters, we have included a few questions that may be helpful for you for personal application or for use in a group setting. We believe there is tremendous value in reading this book with others as a group. Invite some other parents to enter into a dialogue with you and tap into the capacity that you have as a collective group.

By the end of the book, it is our hope that you will …

- rediscover your family's role in a bigger story.
- widen the circles of influence in the lives of your sons and daughters.
- stay focused on what really matters for your children's future.

- renew the fight for your closest relationships.
- create a healthy rhythm in how you interact with one another.
- learn to lead yourself as a parent.

And as a result, we believe you will find ways to parent beyond your capacity.

Reggie Joiner
Carey Nieuwhof

CHAPTER ONE

The Orange Parent

A parent's influence is best realized in partnership with a wider community.

I (Reggie) had two preschoolers before I became aware that I could probably use some help as a parent. I was twenty-eight years old and had just been hired by a large church in Florida as the pastor for young adults and families. The first Sunday after I arrived, we went to lunch after church at a restaurant called Jungle Jim's. As we were escorted to a table in the center of the room, I vividly remember noticing we were surrounded by members of the church who were also having lunch.

We sat at the table and arranged our two children, four-year-old Reggie Paul and two-year-old Hannah. As the new pastor in town, I was sensitive about how well my kids behaved. But before I realized it, the waitress put an orange soda in front of my daughter. Hannah was ecstatic that someone had actually given her something without a lid to drink. She was even more excited when she discovered the designs she could make whenever she flipped her straw and sprayed orange droplets on the white tablecloth.

If you have preschoolers, you know how easy it is for things to get out of your control.

My wife was seated next to Hannah. Sensing my angst, Debbie made a few attempts to redirect our daughter's artistry. With every attempt, Hannah became more determined to decorate the table in orange.

I decided to take things into my own hands. After all, I needed to set an example as a pastor and a parent for an entire congregation now observing the commotion at our table.

Honestly, I'm not sure why I said what I said. I knew better. It was just the only thing I could think of at the time. I was desperate for her to behave. So I leaned in as close to Hannah as I could, stared into her eyes, and said in a voice low enough that only she could hear, "If you touch that straw one more time, you're gonna die!" As a two-year-old, she had already learned how to call my bluff. She glared back at me, looked back at the cup, hit it with her right hand, and poured orange soda all over the table.

I jumped up and grabbed her to make a quick exit for some quality father-daughter conversation. As I walked between the tables, my two-year-old started yelling, "Daddy, please don't kill me! Daddy, please don't kill me!" Then, sensing she had an audience, Hannah kissed me on the cheek and laid her head on my shoulder and said, "Daddy, I'm sorry."

I heard the entire restaurant say with one voice, "Awwww, how sweet."

When I think back to our episode with Hannah's orange soda, I'm reminded of how much more difficult parenting is than most of us realize. Many of us discovered soon after our children were born that our parenting toolboxes were missing some of the tools we needed to be effective at the job.

Many times we found that we had been handed tools from our own parents that we automatically tried to use on our children. It is quite ironic that we will use phrases or techniques that our parents used on us, even though those approaches didn't work on us any better than they work on our kids. I became convinced early in the parenting process that I needed to learn better parenting skills.

In the process, I read hundreds of books, attended dozens of conferences, and had thousands of hours of conversations with parents who were smarter than I was. What did I get out of them? A sinking feeling of being overwhelmed. It seemed like there were dozens of things I needed to improve, and it was difficult to know where to start.

The issue is about my personal capacity. Maybe it's just me, but I never seem to have enough time or space. Instead, my approach to parenting has often been random and reactive. I think many of us respond to what we feel is right in the moment. We reach for the closest book on the shelf, scan the first Web site in our Google search, or sort through multiple lists given to us by the "experts." Then we parent by experiment.

We can always see our mistakes in retrospect better than we realize them in real time. I can mentally search through the archives of our family memories and pinpoint moments I wish I could redo. I poignantly remember times when things got out of control, when my values became clouded and I made decisions based on an immediate situation rather than the big picture. I don't think I am alone. Too many parents wake up one day and realize they have economized on the very relationships they vowed would always be a priority.

Too many parents wake up one day and realize they have economized on the very relationships they vowed would always be a priority.

I recently sat down to summarize a few truths I want to remember about parenting, just so I could stay focused. I'm not suggesting this is a comprehensive list. It is just my own list of parenting priorities:

- What matters more than anything is that my kids have an authentic relationship with God.
- My wife and I are not the only adult influences my children need.
- My children need to know I will never stop fighting for a right relationship with them.
- My relationship with God and with my wife affects my children more than I realize.
- Just *being* together can never substitute for *interacting* together in a meaningful way.

After I wrote these phrases, I realized a common thread ties them together: the value of relationships. Sometimes, we forget the essence of parenting is really about nurturing critical connections that affect every child's future.

At this time in my life, all four of my children are moving through their college years and into adulthood. As I review the past and look forward to what's ahead, I'm amazed how these statements have transcended every season of our experience together. I wish I had written them down twenty years ago. It is just too easy to get preoccupied with trying to be a model parent and forget the real purpose of parenting.

I am going to suggest a few things that I hope you will remember as you read this book:

No one has more potential to influence your child than you.

The fact that you are the primary influence in the life of your child is something you probably already intuitively know. Most parents have a sense that their relationships with their own children are very important. We are aware that we are stewards of influence during the most formative years of someone's life. For good or bad, you will influence your children. This is a responsibility parents carry in a way that no other being on the planet will or should. Teachers, pastors, and coaches will never have as much potential to influence a child's character, self-esteem, perspectives, or faith as a parent does. That teacher, pastor, or coach will have influence that is temporary. It will come and go during different stages of your child's life. Your influence as a parent will be permanent.

Are you starting to feel a little pressure? Good. It may be healthy from time to time to feel a little desperate, especially if your desperation drives you to get help and admit that you don't have the capacity to be a perfect parent. If parenting isn't a little intimidating, then maybe you don't really understand how critical your role is.

Of course, if I really wanted to make you *worry*, I could start quoting the experts and their statistical analyses about everything from high-school dropout rates to teenage pregnancies to juveniles who end up in prison because of bad parenting. I could even show you that if you don't have enough dinners at home with your children, your kids will fly off the tracks.

I would never want to use any of that information to make you panic. If you are like me, you already feel the expectations on parents are pretty lofty. Most of us start off with the bar extremely high. When our first child was born, Debbie and I decided we would never fight in front of our kids, never let them watch television, and never feed them fast food. That was before we realized that the only way we could find time to fight was when they were watching TV and that every McDonald's commercial had subliminal messages that hypnotized our kids to beg for McNuggets. Our standards didn't last very long, and we started feeling guilty early in our parenting experience.

What does all of this have to do with influence? The point is that there is a built-in sense of responsibility most parents feel simply because they are parents. The drive you have to get this right may mistakenly compel you to try to become an expert parent that you will never be. We can buy into the myth that we have to make more lists, get more organized, work much harder, and never make mistakes in order to be successful parents. But instead, we need to remember that our influence has more to do with our relationships with our children than it does our skills as parents. Your purpose as a parent is not to develop exceptional parenting skills.

If you establish unrealistic expectations for yourself, you may create an atmosphere where you become discouraged and frustrate your children. If you are not careful in your zeal to "win" at parenting, you may actually create an unhealthy culture. It is vital to guard your mind-set and stay focused on the primary role of the family.

Your role is not to impress your children or anyone else with your ability to parent; your role is to impress your children with the love and nature of God. The fact that no one has more potential to influence your child than you do implies that you have a natural, God-given advantage to love and lead your children. Does that mean you don't attempt to sharpen and improve your parenting skills? Of course not. But it does mean you parent from the perspective of a relationship, not from your competence or abilities. This levels the playing field for parents. Put another way, this is the reason a mother or father who may not be an expert at communication or a genius in child psychology can be an exceptional parent. Your relationship gives you the potential to influence in a way that others cannot. You are a mother. You are a father. No one else can do what you can do.

That's why Carey and I wrote this book, because we believe in the potential of every parent to do what only he or she can do. But there is a flip side to this principle. It is the other thread that runs through these pages: Some things are simply beyond a parent's capacity to do.

Here is a sobering thought: Your present family will never be enough for your children. Even the best parenting in the best family will never alone be enough to develop relationally, emotionally, and spiritually healthy children. I am not trying to minimize your role, especially when we just finished elevating it. I'm trying to balance it with the polarity of two truths that coexist. The parent is an essential and primary influence. There are things no one can do as well as a parent. But there is another truth that is equally important: There are some things a parent cannot do as well as others. Consider a second principle about influence:

You are not the only influence your children need.

Some parents start out thinking they are the only guidance their kids will need. This starts when children are infants. Then they become preschoolers, and a few years later we discover we have adolescents in the house. We become acutely aware that our kids need something more than just us. It is the process of growth, the path to independence and adulthood. God has designed everyone to need and connect with others. This is central to their significance as they become part of a bigger story and expand their own influence.

When you learn to parent beyond your capacity, you tap into other influences that also have the potential to impact your children's future.

When you learn to parent beyond your capacity, you tap into other influences that also have the potential to impact your children's future. You become intentional about modeling relational values. You exchange short-term outcomes for a long-term impact. Here is a primary point of this book: Your children one day will seek affirmation and approval from adults other than you. Either you can become intentional about enlisting other trusted adults to influence your kids, or you can depend only on your limited capacity. You can leave them alone to discover random influences who will shape their character and faith, or you can help them proactively pursue strategic relationships for their lives.

This principle has a direct correlation to your capacity. Face it. Your children will encounter a number of things that you are not skilled at doing. Maybe it's in the area of education, health, athletics, or talents. Just because you may not possess a specific skill does not mean that you don't have the relational influence to move your son or daughter to get whatever help he or she needs. Isn't that what parents do all the time? If you don't have the skill, you take the initiative to tap into something beyond your ability. You enlist a tutor, teacher, coach, doctor, or nurse to help. With a strong commitment to do what you can and to seek out the help of others to do what you can't, you practice a version of parenting beyond your present capacity. It's not your ability or skill level that matters as much as it is your relationships with your kids and your efforts to move them in the right direction.

What if you simply admitted that you don't have enough capacity on your own to raise your son or daughter?

What would happen if you decided to become intentional about inviting other leaders into your children's lives?

This is where a third principle comes into the picture:

Two combined influences will make a greater impact than just two influences.

We call that the Orange Factor.

If you haven't experienced it already, you will almost certainly encounter finger painting during your child's preschool years. A magical moment occurs when a child learns that mixing two colors produces something new. It is exciting to see how two pigments can merge to create something different and distinctive. That's what happens when red and yellow combine their efforts to make orange.

We use the color orange to symbolize what it means to parent beyond your capacity. It is just one way to visually remind parents why they need other influences in the lives of children. If you trust someone else to help teach your daughter math, you are thinking Orange. If you depend on a coach to show your son how to throw a football, you are thinking Orange. You are tapping into another influence besides your own to make a greater impact. What if we applied the same principle to the moral and spiritual development of our children? What if we assigned the color red to represent the unconditional love of family, and what if yellow represented the light that comes from a larger community of faith? When those two influences combine efforts to influence a child, the result is transformational.

Carey and I have seen firsthand the role other Christian leaders play in the lives of our children. So when we think Orange, this color reminds us of the importance of a partnership between parents and the church. Both are important, and the principle is simple. If you paint only with red, you will see

When you think Orange, you see that two combined influences make a greater impact than just two influences.

what only red can do. If you paint only with yellow, you will see what only yellow can do. But when you paint with red and yellow, you'll get new possibilities, fresh solutions, vibrant outcomes. When you think Orange, you see that two combined influences make a greater impact than just two influences.

Hopefully, you are beginning to see the potential.

There are two powerful influences on the planet—
the church and the home.

They both exist because God initiated them.
They both exist because God desires to use them
to demonstrate His plan of redemption and restoration.

If they work together they can potentially
make a greater impact than if they work alone.
They need each other.

Too much is at stake for either one to fail.
Their primary task is to build God's kingdom
in the hearts of men and women, sons and daughters.

Both the family and the church are systems comprised of imperfect people but designed by God to tell His story to the world. When you think Orange, you embrace the potential of combining your influence with that of a faith community to make a greater impact than either of you can make on your own.

We are not simply suggesting you just find a church to make your children more spiritual. That would still be only painting yellow. And it's going to take

Working on the same thing at the same time is not as effective as working on the same thing at the same time

more than your family has to offer. That would be only painting red. Your family and church are probably trying to do the best job they can independently. Churches are full of programs that inspire families, and countless families participate regularly in their local churches. Both groups are simultaneously hard at work to build faith in children, but in most cases they are not working in sync. They may be working toward a similar goal, but working on the same thing at the same time is not as effective as working on the same thing at the same time *with the same strategy.* When you creatively synchronize the two environments, you get more than just red or yellow—you tap into the Orange Factor.

Our hope is that this book will help you know how to partner with the right influences to make a greater impact in your kids' lives. Throughout the following pages we want to help you clarify the shared values we believe will help you prioritize the relationships that will shape your children's future.

We are going to invite you to engage your family in a bigger story, a story that will expand their perspectives and reveal a significant role in this world. It's a story that involves more than just your family; it involves other influences who are on a journey to discover who God is and why a relationship with Him really matters. We hope the essential values in this book will help you navigate through a variety of different seasons as a parent. We want to encourage you to establish a lifestyle as a parent where you ...

> *Widen the Circle* ... Invite others to invest in your children, so your sons and daughters have other voices that will help shape and determine the direction of their lives.

> *Imagine the End* ... Focus your energy and effort on the issues that will make a lasting impact.

> *Fight for the Heart* ... Create a culture of unconditional love in your home to fuel the emotional and moral health of your children.

> *Create a Rhythm* ... Tap into the power of quality moments together, and build a sense of purpose through your everyday experiences.

> *Make It Personal* ... Allow your kids to see how you strive to grow so they can understand how to confront their own limitations and pursue character and faith.

Each of these values can help you establish a lifestyle of parenting beyond your capacity. Here is what we promise will happen if you read this book:

- You will still get tired as a parent.
- You will still struggle with what you should do in a number of situations.
- Your kids will still not always behave exactly the way you want.
- You will still stay awake sometimes, worrying about your kids.
- You will still wonder, more than you should, if you're a good parent.

Oh, and there's one more thing we promise ...

> Your relationship with your children,
> and with the other people they need in their lives,
> will move in a better direction.

CHAPTER TWO

Stock Family Syndrome

God isn't holding up a perfect picture; He's writing a bigger story.

When it comes to parenting, how are you feeling? Is your family the picture you had in mind? The truth is, we are all holding pictures of what we think a family is supposed to be. Our pictures come from a variety of sources: traditional images, media, parenting books, Hollywood, and many other places.

Maybe church is where you got your picture of the ideal family. Your church might even have a message series every year that says your home should look something like this: Dad's in charge, you have breakfast devotionals every morning, you pray together every night, you listen to contemporary Christian music in the car, you have framed verses on the walls, you stay neatly within biblical roles as husband and wife, you vote conservatively, and you tithe 10 percent of your gross

We all have an image of family.

income. In this house, children get up every morning and call their parents blessed.

We all have an image of family. You have learned from the pictures around you, and you are holding a mental impression of what you think your family should look like. You are confronted with images in the mall and movie theater, on church brochures and billboards, at the doctors' and dentists' offices. Everywhere you go, you are reminded of how ideal families dress and act. For just a moment, take a closer look at one of the model families that some of us aspire to become.

They're the Stock family: Rob and Allison Stock and their two children, Tyler and Emma. He's clean-cut, wearing a name-brand shirt and expensive jeans. Her hair is long, her smile is endearing, and her teeth are white and straight. Tyler is two and a half years older than Emma, and they hold the door for each other every time they enter a room. The sun is shining, and a picnic basket sits just outside of camera range.

The perfect family, wouldn't you say?

So many times our focus becomes the picture we have created of a certain kind of family. We build up the Stock family as though every family ought to be like them.

And everything's great until we realize the Stock family isn't a real family.

They are what their name implies: a stock image from a photo bank. They've been Photoshopped. They're just four attractive models who were paid to do a photo shoot so shopping malls, clothing stores, grocery chains, and even churches can use their image to create the illusion of something that doesn't actually exist.

Of course, the Stock photo does just what it's designed to do. It portrays a picture of a perfect life and creates dissatisfaction about our own life circumstances.

In the real world, though, the Stocks may be quite different from that photo. Rob might be a pharmacist battling a prescription drug addiction, and Allison is increasingly depressed because of their credit card debt. Tyler suffers from ADHD, and Emma is in therapy after she was caught tearing the heads off her Barbie dolls.

None of that is true, of course. But it is true that *this* story is much closer to reality than what the stock image portrays. It's closer to where most families actually live.

Reality looks different for every family.

Reality looks different for every family. Maybe it's an addiction. Perhaps an affair or a divorce. Or an out-of-control son or daughter.

For many of us it might be less dramatic, a weariness that comes from living in the tension of sharing the same square footage with people you say you love. Or maybe the fatigue stems from the stress of career dissatisfaction, a marriage that has gone flat, too many nights out with the kids at soccer, or the sheer boredom of the suburbs.

For others, it's an uninvited guest that shatters family life—an illness or an accident, someone gets fired, *something* goes wrong. Regardless, what you hoped for is no longer what you are living.

But the common denominator is this: We are left holding an image of family we will never be able to realize. We look at the Stocks and say, "*That's not us* … but we still feel an incredible pressure for it to *be* us."

We're steeped in the reality of family life.

Family is messy.

Parenting is hard.

There is no single model.

A lot of families and parents don't fit so neatly in this Stock photo. For most of us, *real* is much closer to home than *ideal*.

We're thinking of Hadley and Amy Brandt. Hadley worked for Apple for fourteen years and is the architect behind most of our reThink Web structure. This is the second marriage for both Hadley and Amy. Hadley adopted Amy's five-year-old son, then they had two more kids together, Nate and Kelsey. I'm not sure they would fit with some people's pictures, but they are a real family. You could hold up a picture of a perfect family next to them, but it wouldn't make a lot of sense in their context.

We also think of Bouavanh and Paul, who own the restaurant next to our office space in Atlanta. The restaurant is called Mommy Francis, and they've got great food, including fried pickles you'd write home about. We've become good friends over the past few years. They met when Bouavanh was thirteen and Paul was seventeen. Bouavanh is from Laos. Paul is African-American. They've been living together for nearly twenty years, and they have two daughters: River and Tsunami. (Paul says his girls can't date until they're at least sixteen.) You could show them a photo of what some would say a perfect family looks like, but I just don't think it would translate. Still, from their perspective, they're a real family, and that's what matters to them.

Consider Troy and Karen Smith. They adopted Haley when she was five. Haley's mother was a teenage mom, and her dad wasn't really in the picture. Haley grew up with Troy and Karen, who are actually her grandparents. Haley has a great story and is a gifted musician who loves to work with inner-city girls. If you were to ask Troy and Karen if everything worked out the way they pictured, they'd probably say no. Theirs was not the ideal picture, but their story is powerful.

We wish you could get to know Corey Brailsford. He and his mom, Nadine, were in a terrible auto accident when he was just four years old. Even though he had his seat belt buckled, Corey was tragically injured and has lived as a paraplegic since his preschool years. His story of survival and triumph is inspiring, but Nadine is quick to say that she never expected her family photo to turn out this way. Imagine confronting the Brailsfords with an idealistic stock photo of what a family should look like. It will never be a picture they can achieve, but that doesn't mean they're not a family.

Our friends Chrystina and Jayce Fincher have a good perspective on this issue. Jayce was in a band that got to number five on the Billboard rock charts. But the industry lifestyle was hard on Jayce and even more difficult for his marriage. Jayce and Chrystina almost didn't make it, but Jayce decided to walk away from his popularity and music in a desperate attempt to restore his relationship with his family. If you had talked to Chrystina, she would have told you it just wasn't the picture she expected her marriage to be … it wasn't the dream she had at her wedding. She almost left, but she didn't. The point is that if Chrystina had been too preoccupied with a perfect picture, the real-life picture of Jayce, Chrystina, and their three kids (Holden, Ava, and Cashman) may not have even existed. If you were to hold up the stock family to the Finchers, they might say, *That just isn't who we are, or who we will ever be … but we are a real family.*

These families may never make it into a church brochure or parenting magazine, but nevertheless something amazing is happening in their lives.

Some well-meaning Christians are tempted to confront these families and suggest that what they need is a biblical approach to parenting. After all, biblical characters must have been exemplary parents.

Well, hang on. When you actually go back to the Bible, the parenting examples you encounter might surprise you. They are not what you may expect:

NOAH had a drinking problem.

ABRAHAM offered his wife to another man.

REBEKAH schemed with her son to deceive her husband, Isaac.

JACOB's sons sold their brother into slavery.

DAVID had an affair, and his son started a rebellion.

ELI lost total control of how his boys acted in church.

You say, "What about Joseph and Mary? They raised Jesus, and He turned out okay." That's true, but don't forget the time they left Him at church for three days. Today, they would have been reported to child services. Adam and Eve might have been good examples had they not single-handedly caused the downfall of the human race and subsequently raised one son who killed the other.

That's biblical family. As you read the Bible, you begin to realize the afternoon talk shows would have had an ample supply of guests from its pages.

Be honest: If most of the parents in the Bible had shown up in your church, you would have suggested they go to counseling. Immediately. You surely wouldn't have wanted them to be spiritual leaders.

If most of the parents in the Bible had shown up in your church, you would have suggested they go to counseling.

No one is dismissing "religious" parents, but neither can we assert that the Bible offers paragons of parenting. The Bible lends advice about parenting, including a number of universal principles we should apply, but you would have a hard time convincing us that David or Noah or even Joseph was an exceptional parent.

God's Story

Clearly, God is not trying to paint a picture of an ideal family. I sometimes wonder if God included bad examples of parenting in the Bible to give the rest of us hope.

So what is He doing?

He's not trying to give you a better picture.

He's writing a story.

It's a story with multiple chapters, a story that's unfolding, a story that is a process, not a point in time. A story with multiple opportunities as you go along—not a snapshot, but a plotline in which God desires to reveal Himself over and over again.

God's story is a story in which everyday faith becomes a reality. A story where we have a chance to redefine our relationships. A way to start again. It's a story that gives every family and every parent a chance. *If God can use them … then maybe there's hope for me.*

People often wonder why stories from the Bible are so conflicted, violent, and difficult. Honestly, that may be something to give thanks for. It means God is actually engaged in *our* world, not some imaginary one. God is writing a story in real lives, in real time, in real ways.

It seems like God is more interested in using broken people than He is in creating a better picture.

The Bible demonstrates with surprising candor that God is interested in using broken people to tell His story. In fact, according to Scripture, broken people are the very best ones to tell the story of God. Broken people are the primary characters featured in almost every story.

It seems like God is more interested in using broken people than He is in creating a better picture.

It's as though God is saying, *I'm going to use churches and families, both composed of broken people, as platforms to demonstrate to the world that I am a God of restoration and redemption.*

We can breathe a little easier to learn that God is not nearly as interested in putting a picture in *front* of us as much He is trying to tell a story *through* us.

Your Family Story

Too many of us buy into the myth that we need to become the right kind of parent before God can use us. In reality, God is longing to tell His story through our imperfections and brokenness.

If you were to invite God into your less-than-ideal story and learn to cooperate with whatever He wants to do in your life, the dynamic of your family could radically change.

If you were to invite God into your less-than-ideal story and learn to cooperate with whatever He wants to do in your life, the dynamic of your family could radically change. If your picture is not where you want it to be at this time, you may be tempted to throw in the towel. Don't focus on the picture. Focus instead on the bigger story God desires to illustrate through you.

Rather than painting a picture of a perfect family, God wants to use family as a canvas for His redemptive story. He wants to use the family to show us what it means to have an authentic, everyday faith with a God who redeems and restores broken people.

Degrees of Dysfunction

The truth is, there is a degree of dysfunction in every family. After all, a family is merely a gathering of flawed human beings. It's easy for us as parents to get discouraged, especially if we have been trying to *fix* the family. History is not on our side. But what if our job is *not* to fix the family so we all look like some retouched picture? What if our purpose as parents is to illuminate the bigger story, to influence the next generation to experience God in a more genuine way?

Consider this: If you become preoccupied with the Stock family, it is easy to fall into a trap where …

- you feel like you never measure up. (It may even be the reason you drop out of church.)
- you lose credibility with other parents who recognize the difference in what you are and what you claim to be. (It may be the reason some of your friends never come to church.)
- you discourage other parents with a standard they can never achieve. (This may be the reason parents give up and disconnect from the places where they can find the resources they need most.)

Parenting is intimidating enough. If we raise the bar to levels that not even the Bible itself portrays, in what way does that possibly help families? Unrealistic pictures paralyze parents. Those unyielding demands cause families to lose hope. Our experience has been that when parents become preoccupied with ideal pictures, it can actually do the opposite of expanding their capacity: It will drain their energy. Better Picture thinking can devastate your heart as a parent and handicap the future hope of your children. But focusing on the story God wants to tell and pointing to a bigger context of life ignites faith and possibility.

Two Different Approaches

What we are suggesting is that there are two different approaches to family.

When we take the Better Picture approach, we try to conform every family to our picture of what family should be.

When we take the Bigger Story approach, we learn to see every family as a potential platform for God to demonstrate His story of redemption and restoration.

This requires a shift in thinking. It changes the way you see yourself as a parent. It transforms the way you see other parents and families, both inside and outside the church.

There is a phrase I (Reggie) wrote down late one night to remind myself what is really important. It keeps me going when I feel like I am not doing great as a parent. It is also a reminder to me of how I need to see every parent and family I meet:

> God is at work telling a story of restoration and redemption through your family. No matter what your family looks like or how limited your capacity might be, you can cooperate with whatever God desires to do in your heart so your children will have a front-row seat to the grace and goodness of God.

What if you really started believing that God has a bigger story for every parent?

Those of you who are married
Those of you who have never been married

Those of you who are remarried
Those of you who are divorced

Those of you who have adopted children
Those who have assumed responsibility
for one of your children's children

Those of you who live in your dream neighborhood
Those of you who live in a one-room apartment
Those of you who don't have anywhere to live

Those of you who feel trapped by a financial crisis
Those of you who are impaired by health limitations
Those of you who have been abused by someone you loved

Those of you who go to church
Those of you who don't go to church

Those of you who believe in God
Those of you who have never believed in God
Those of you who believed and stopped believing
Those of you who have no idea what to believe

What if you simply decided to start looking at your family through the context of a bigger story? What if you purposed, regardless of your situation, to become a living demonstration of how something that is broken can be restored? What if you invited your children into a bigger story, instead of encouraging them to conform to a superficial ideal? Then maybe you will begin to have renewed potential as a parent to give your children a lasting sense of hope. You will gain fresh opportunities to affect the way your children see their future. You can begin to impact how your children embrace an everyday faith, understand their purpose, and pursue right relationships. When you add a bigger-story perspective to your children's world, you add something that goes far beyond your capacity as a parent.

God sees family in the context of that much bigger story. Alone, we can only do so much. Our capacity will be pressed to its limits. But God knows our limits, and He has already set in place a plan for us to parent beyond our weaknesses, our situations, and our human-ness. This plan isn't new, but it does require a fresh perspective on our part, to begin to see how God through time and space has used the family to demonstrate an eternal story of unconditional love and grace.

The family exists, even in its imperfection, to display the heart of God to every generation.

The Bible does not give us an ideal picture of the family, but it does suggest that every father, mother, and child has a unique role in portraying God's love to one another. The family exists, even in its imperfection, to display the heart of God to every generation.

I used to wonder why so much genealogy was included in the Bible. The genealogies don't have a lot of profound revelations, and they don't seem to be very relevant to my daily life. However, I realize now that these lists display family after family and generation after generation to show that every family and every generation was connected to God's story.

You can see the continuation of God's redemptive plan as it unfolds in the Hebrew family tree from Adam to Jesus, from Genesis to the Gospels. Maybe these lists are there to remind us that God is actively using families to link the past to the future so that they might broadcast His love to every generation. The family was and is God's primary conduit. He has used families—mothers and fathers, daughters and sons—as a timeless platform throughout history to put His glory on display. In the Old Testament, God's promises and commandments were passed from one generation to the next through families. The heart of God was communicated primarily through the heart of the family.

Although the concept of family has had different expressions over time, it has always been significant. Governments are organized, walls are built, and battles are fought for the sake of families. It is the core of civilization and a primary influence on the human condition. Family has shaped the fabric of the social, religious, and political structures of every society. The heart of the family affects the direction of every child and the future of every nation. For centuries, kings and queens, presidents and senates, pastors and priests have attempted to address and resolve issues concerning families, because every wise leader knows that whatever happens in the family makes an impression on the world.

One leader from the Old Testament understood this particularly well. He was appointed to govern an entire race of people who had been severely oppressed. The people had suffered hundreds of years of persecution. Their identity as a race had been threatened, their will crushed, and their faith assaulted. In a legendary rescue attempt, this leader became the strategic influence that saved the entire nation from probable genocide. He helped them rediscover their distinctiveness as a people and rebuild their faith.

Their transition to healing and recovery took them through several decades, hundreds of miles, and countless challenges. The entire race endured an agonizing process in preparation for redeeming its heritage.

After years of waiting, the day approached when these people would reclaim their homeland and settle their families in their native country. Suddenly, rumors spread throughout the nation that the leader was stepping down. The people were aghast, thinking he had come too far not to complete the journey with them. He had become their patriarch, a hero to their children. He had rescued and revived their destiny as a people. This was their pivotal moment. They were on the brink of their most promising days.

They gathered tentatively to listen to his farewell speech. He began by recounting their journey and reminding them of the covenants they had made with their God. They had heard all of this before, and for a while it seemed as if he was simply reviewing what they already knew.

Then he subtly began to shift his message. In his voice and words, they could hear a new and unexpected concern about their future. They had been ecstatic about finally arriving at their promised destination, yet he seemed anxious about how their newfound blessings might affect their faith. More specifically, he seemed intent on addressing how they would transfer their faith to their children and the generations to come.

Too much was at stake to let this fall by the wayside. It had taken a long time to get to this point, and he wanted to ensure they didn't make the same mistakes many of their parents had made. Then he said something profoundly different from anything he had ever said before, challenging every listener:

> *Hear, O Israel: The LORD our God, the LORD is one. Love the LORD your God with all your heart and with all your soul and with all your strength. These commandments that I give you today are to be upon your hearts. Impress them on your children. Talk about them when you sit at home and when you walk along the road, when you lie down and when you get up. Tie them as symbols on your hands and bind them on your foreheads. Write them on the doorframes of your houses and on your gates.*

> *When the LORD your God brings you into the land He swore to your fathers, to Abraham, Isaac, and Jacob, to give you—a land with large, flourishing cities you did not build, houses filled with all kinds of good things you did not provide, wells you did not dig, and vineyards and olive groves you did not plant—then when you eat and are satisfied, be careful that you do not forget the LORD, who brought you out of Egypt, out of the land of slavery.*[1]

Deuteronomy documents the message Moses gave to the Israelites before he died, just before they took possession of the

Promised Land. Moses is transitioning his leadership to Joshua, giving his farewell address regarding the critical issues facing Israel's future. As a seasoned, one-hundred-twenty-year-old leader, Moses warns the Hebrew people against the danger of becoming spoiled by the wealth of Canaan.

He admonishes them to "be careful" not to forget God, because he knows how easy it will be for them to get distracted by prosperity and riches. He gives them a plan to guard their heritage and transfer their faith to the next generation. Moses' words are deliberate and strategic for anyone interested in leaving a legacy.

In a pivotal moment in Israel's history, this leader speaks to the entire nation and calls everyone to be responsible for how the next generation will be raised. No one is excluded from the circle. His comments have incredible insights for all parents about their roles in influencing their children's relationships with God.

Within this passage from Deuteronomy 6 are values that help families shepherd the responsibility they have to transmit an everyday faith to their sons and daughters. The Hebrew people had just come through an encounter with God that was filled with wonder, discovery, and passion. And in light of a more affluent life ahead for the

Moses realized that God chose the family and the faith community as the two entities through which He would tell His story to a generation.

people of Israel, Moses was determined to ensure that the next generation had a faith as practical and dynamic as the current generation.

Again, Moses realized that God chose the family and the faith community as the two entities through which He would tell His story to a generation. We could restate it this way:

Churches are made up of broken people.

Families are made up of broken people.

Both exist for the same reason: to show a broken world God's message of restoration and redemption.

That's why God set up a framework for parents and leaders to work together around a synchronized plan to help children grow morally and spiritually. We believe that framework and the values within it speak as powerfully today as they did three thousand years ago. In the next five chapters, we'll explore those values and how they can help parents today win at home.

Are you ready? Rather than hoping for an ideal picture, it's time to join a movement of parents who are letting God write a bigger story.

Stock Family Syndrome

DISCUSSION QUESTIONS

1. Describe your vision of the "perfect family." Where did your idea of the perfect family come from? How does your family measure up to your vision?

2. Do you put pressure on yourself and your family to become this "perfect family" image?

3. How does the image of what you think you are *supposed* to be affect the way you parent your children?

4. What are some things about your family that you consider less than ideal? How do you think God feels about the imperfections of your family?

5. Based on what you have read in this chapter, how does God *really* feel about your family? How does the way you view God impact the way you view and lead your family?

6. How have you seen God show up in the happy times of your family? How about in the heartbreaking times?

7. How might the way you see your family change if you started to have the perspective of God's bigger story, redeeming and restoring your family for His purposes?

CHAPTER THREE ↑

Family Value #I: Widen the Circle

Pursue strategic relationships for your kids.

If you understand the physics behind using a lever of any kind, you have a visual of what it means to do something beyond your capacity. A lever enables you to move or lift something that would ordinarily exceed your ability. The word *lever* comes from a French word that means "to raise." When you use a lever, you typically exert whatever force you can on your end of the lever, and this effort magnifies energy on the other end. Basically you do your part, and the lever enhances your influence to make a greater impact.

Imagine for just a moment that you have three levers you could move to elevate the influences that affect your child's life. Suppose each lever has a different function, but they are all extremely important to

Imagine for just a moment that you have three levers you could move to elevate the influences that affect your child's life.

the future of your son or daughter. Collectively the levers represent the primary influences that will determine how your children see themselves, how they view the world, how they make decisions, how they relate to people. These levers can ultimately affect the direction of your children's lives. Although you don't have the capacity to directly impact everything that happens to your child, you do have the capacity to do your part, to apply energy to your side of the lever.

The Three Levers

In the coming chapters we will talk about the lever you use to *enhance your child's relationship with you*. At times you are sensitive enough to know that your kids need more of your attention. So you leverage your time with them. This happens when you make it a priority to be physically and emotionally present. It also is a result of communicating consistently with your children in a way that fights for their hearts. When you create a rhythm and use teachable moments to speak into their lives, you are leveraging your relational experiences to bond and build memories that fuel their emotions. When you manage this lever, you ensure that there will be a quantity of quality times in your home that will build a lasting friendship and a healthy relationship between you and your children.

The second lever is in some ways even more critical than the first. If you want to tap into unlimited capacity, you use whatever human ability you have to move this lever. It is the lever that *advances your child's relationship with God.* No one has the potential to move this lever like you do. As the parent, you are the one who can monitor their hearts, their character, and their faith. You are also the one who has the best potential to model what the unconditional love of a heavenly Father looks like. When you activate this lever, you nudge them toward their own relationship with a God who has an unlimited capacity to love them. As you apply this lever you recognize that their relationship with God is even more important than their relationship with you. You are guiding them toward an eternal relationship that will give them the ability to navigate through an uncertain future with hope.

There is also a third lever. It is similar to the first two in that it has to do with a key relationship as well. As your children get older, this lever becomes more and more important. Some experts even suggest that during the teenage years, this third one may be the best one you can leverage to influence their direction. As your direct personal influence with your children evolves in late adolescence, this lever becomes increasingly important. This chapter is about the lever that *connects your child to relationships with those outside your home.*

The importance of this third lever became very evident to me (Reggie) when my son, Reggie Paul, turned sixteen. As father and son we had always had a positive relationship, significant moments together, and lots of conversations about faith. He was integrally involved with our church. But somewhere during his second year of high school, things began to change.

As he shifted toward a certain group of friends and became more independent, he and I were both taken by surprise at the strain that began to show up in our relationship. We were going through a real tug-of-war, and it was all connected to—you might guess—a girl he was dating.

I remember thinking his years of experience with me as his father would make him pay more attention to me than to a girl he *just met*. But I was wrong. I couldn't compete. It all exploded one night when he came home past curfew, and I walked into his room to confront him.

I said, "You are late coming home from a date, and I just need to know what's going on."

He replied, "Dad, I don't really want to talk to you about it."

"Well, you don't have an option," I explained. "I need you to tell me everything that went on tonight, and I need you to tell me now."

He looked at me as if I were a stranger and said, "No. I'm not going to tell you that."

Then I did something that came naturally. I moved the first lever and said, "RP, this is me. You know I care about you. I need you to tell me what's going on because I am your father."

Then he said something that caught me off guard. None of my children had ever said it before. It was gutsy. It was honest. But it shocked me. "No, you don't understand, Dad. I'm not going to tell you *because* you are my father. You make the rules."

I just wasn't ready for that response. I was flustered. I didn't know what to do. That night I told my wife, Debbie, "If he can't talk to me because I make the rules, then I am not sure I want to make the rules anymore."

The next day, I showed up at my friend Andy Stanley's office and said, "I just don't understand. I'm trying to get my son to tell me what's going on, and he won't tell me anything."

Andy thought for a second, then with a twitch of sarcasm said to me, "Well, did *you* tell *your* father everything?"

I muttered, "No, but what does that have to do with anything?"

The next day I went back to Reggie Paul. I said, "Andy told me that you ought to tell me everything you're doing because that's what a good son would do."

No, actually, that's not what I said. I said, "I talked to Andy, and he said he didn't tell his father everything either, and I should understand why you won't tell me everything. I'm trying to be okay with that. But I do need to ask you a different question." It was then that I learned for the first time the power of the third lever. I asked my son, "If you won't tell me, then who will you tell?"

His response was easy. He said, "That's fair. I'll tell you who. I'll talk to Kevin." As soon as he said Kevin's name, I felt a huge sense of relief because Kevin had been a family friend for years. I knew he loved our family, respected me, and had the same values we had. I remember thinking that Kevin would be a very safe place to go.

I knew then more than ever before what a gift it was for me to have this other adult in my son's life. I didn't worry about what Kevin would tell Reggie Paul because I knew he would be saying the same kinds of things that I would say.

Let's rewind the conversation back to the second day in my son's bedroom to when I asked him, "If you won't tell me, then who will you tell?" What if there had not been a Kevin in his life? What if at this defining moment the best he could give me was a shrugged shoulder or an "I don't know"?

I am fortunate to have participated in a church for most of my life where it is easy to move the third lever, where men and

When you ask, "Who are you going to talk to?" would your kids have a name?

women invest in the lives of kids and teenagers because they believe it is important to widen the circle.

What if you were to have a conversation with your teenage son or daughter? When you ask, "Who are you going to talk to?" would your kids have a name? Would they identify a trusted adult in their lives who would give them a safe place to wrestle with difficult issues?

Regardless of your stage of parenting, I can promise you one thing:

> *A time will come when you and your children will need another adult in their lives besides you.*

We encourage parents to start moving a lever to widen the circle as soon as they can. We train church leaders to organize their ministries to put small-group leaders in the lives of kids as early as preschool. Why? Because we want to make sure parents recognize the value of having other trusted leaders in the lives of their kids as they grow up.

It is easy for us to send the wrong signals to our children when they need objective voices in their lives. The more I thought about what Reggie Paul said to me that day, the more it made sense.

He had a reason when he said, "I'm not going to tell you *because* you are my father. You make the rules." He was not simply implying that he was worried about what I would do if I found out. It goes deeper than that. Other things were playing out in his mind as a sixteen-year-old. It was as if he was saying, "You are too close, you care too much, you are too connected to me. There is the potential with this issue that you could be more emotional than reasonable. You can't be as rational as you need to be, and the reason you can't is because I am your son and you are my dad. I need someone at this moment with a different kind of objectivity."

He needed more than a PARENT. He needed somebody who cared about him but who was not responsible for him. He needed somebody who would say what I would say as his parent but who didn't make the rules.

He needed more than a COMPANION his own age. He needed someone who had been down that road and could look back and say, "You need to watch out for *this* and make sure you go *that* direction."

Sometimes moving this lever can be difficult for a parent. I know I have learned a couple of really important things.

First of all, *don't take it too personally.*

You need to accept that you will not always be the one your children run to. As a matter of fact, if you try too hard to be that person, you might be the one they run away from.

Second, *don't be too proud.*

An element of this makes every parent a little nervous. I'm no different. The idea that our kids will confide in someone else about what's going on in their heads is one thing. The possibility they might get honest about what's going on in their homes could be embarrassing to me personally. Give your kids permission to express themselves in a safe place, even if it's a little awkward for you as a parent. It would be better for someone who cares about your family to have insider information than someone who doesn't. Choose to be more concerned about what your kids need as your children than about how you look as a parent.

Here's the main question: *What are you doing to encourage your child's relationships with people outside the home?* This is a powerful principle that we cannot miss as parents.

When I hear people talk about Deuteronomy 6, they often rush right by something important at the beginning. It's in the phrase, *"Hear, O Israel."* It's what I would call the covert context of the passage. Moses is speaking to *all* of Israel about the importance of families passing on their faith to the next generation. He was talking to every parent *and* everyone else. We assume because there is so much language about family and children that he was talking primarily to parents, but Moses was speaking to *all* of Israel. The culture of the Israelites was that of a community. Not only were parents listening, but there were others in the crowd as well: aunts, uncles, grandparents, and a wider circle of adults.

The Hebrew culture described in Deuteronomy naturally promoted this kind of relationship. We're challenged to rethink our understanding of family, as the Fuller Youth Institute explains: "A family in the Old Testament would have included parents, children, workers, perhaps adult siblings with their own spouses and children. In fact, households could be compiled of as many as eighty people. These texts, such as Deuteronomy 6, are discussing the communal raising of children. Our own cultural distance from these passages may cause us to put undue pressure on parents alone."[1]

The family unit then was not always as neatly defined as we sometimes think. Regardless of how you would describe that ancient system, one thing is definitely true: The system offered significant multigenerational support for parents. I think the reason Moses would say things about "you, your children and their children after them"[2] is because all those generations were represented in the crowd.

How do we rediscover the principle of wider-circle community that existed in the Hebrew story? How do we rally parents and churches to see how strategic they are in nurturing the hearts of children?

As a parent, I believe that one of the greatest values of the church is its potential to provide community for my children. I want my children and teenagers to know that the church is a place where they can show up and be safe, a place where they can have meaningful dialogue with another trusted adult, and a place where they can ask difficult questions.

Widening the circle involves pursuing strategic relationships for your son or daughter.

In a culture where community is not automatic and there are limited role models, parents should become intentional about finding spiritual leaders and mentors for their kids. Every son and daughter needs other adults in their lives who will say things that reflect what a parent would say. One of the smartest things moms and dads can do is to participate in a church where they can find the right kind of adult influences for their kids.

Here is a piece of research that might interest some of you as parents:

> Teens who had at least one adult from church make a significant time investment in their lives …

were more likely to keep attending church. More of those who stayed in church—by a margin of 46 percent to 28 percent—said five or more adults at church had invested time with them personally and spiritually.[3]

I have observed a lot of teenagers. From the time they hit middle school, they start moving away from home. They are not doing anything wrong; it's just the way they are made. They are becoming independent, and they begin redefining themselves through the eyes of other people who are not in their immediate family.

The older they get, the more important it is for them to have other voices in their lives saying the same things but in a different way. Teenage sons and daughters need to have other voices speaking into their worlds.

Parents who do not understand this principle have forgotten what it was like to be a teenager. I cannot count the times my kids would quote something a teacher, our student pastor, or a coach had said. They would act like it was the first time they had ever heard it. I wanted to blurt out, "I have been telling you that for sixteen years!" They were hearing it in a different way because they were at a different stage, and they just needed a different voice.

Widening the circle transitions your child from a "me" approach to a "we" approach.

When you widen the circle, you not only recognize the need for others to influence your children but also the need for your children to be a part of something that is much larger than just your family. A wider circle gives them not only a place to belong, but a significant role to engage in the bigger story we talked about in the last chapter.

Seth Godin makes this observation: "Human beings can't help it; we need to belong. One of the most powerful of our survival mechanisms is to be part of a tribe, to contribute to (and take from) a group of like-minded people."[4]

The right community is not only important because of what it gives to your children, but also because of what it requires from your children.

Don't miss this point. The right community is not only important because of what it gives to your children, but also because of what it requires from your children. Children need more than just a family that gives them unconditional acceptance and love; they need a tribe that gives them a sense of belonging and significance. The concept of church in the New Testament was never intended to simply be something your children attend. Church should be defined as a vibrant community that engages your children to demonstrate God's love to a broken world. When parents and leaders synchronize around this aspect of a wider circle, it has the potential to mobilize a child's faith from something that is static to something that is dynamic.

In *Inside Out Families,* Diana Garland reports on her study of what makes the most impact in a student's spiritual life. She concludes after extensive surveys and research, "Community service was significantly more closely related to the faith development of teens than attending worship services. Service appears to be more powerful than Sunday school, Bible study, or participation in worship in the faith development of teenagers."[5]

She goes on to document that when teens serve alongside adults, the experience broadens their faith and redefines their understanding of church.

We recently asked a group of seasoned leaders from around the country this question about spiritual development: "If you had six ninth-grade boys or girls for four years, what would you do to encourage their spiritual development?" They each talked about different work projects and mission endeavors. Some mentioned the amount of time they would devote to building the relationship. Some brought up authors they would want to read together. Toward the end of the conversation, we realized that no one had brought up taking them to any kind of classroom presentation. Although these leaders guide churches with a large array of programs, not one suggested just putting teens into classes or trying to simply get them to attend church. Instinctively, many leaders recognize something more relational and experiential required for spiritual formation. What if *that's* the kind of experience that student ministries facilitated for kids? What if that's what church became for young people?

Actually the approach they described seemed similar to what Jesus did with His twelve disciples over two thousand years ago. Jesus did not teach the disciples to do ministry. He did ministry with the disciples while He taught them.

Something powerful happens when you partner with other influences who desire to instill a sense of mission into the hearts of your children. You give them a different view of their place in the world, and you transfer a different kind of passion to them that your family alone cannot give them. It doesn't mean that you as parents can't engage in this mission with them. You should attempt to let your kids see what God can do through your family, as well as leverage influences to show them what God can do through them personally.

I (Carey) always knew there was a passage into manhood that was supposed to take place, but I had no idea how it happened. My son Jordan and I talked about it, and when he turned thirteen we set up what we refer to as his mentoring year. Early in the year, we sat down and selected five men in our relational circle that we both knew and felt comfortable with. I approached each man and explained what we were doing.

The plan was fairly simple. I asked each mentor to spend one day with Jordan over the summer. They could do whatever they wanted to do, and over the course of the day, I asked each mentor to impart one spiritual truth (something faith-based) and one life truth (good advice). I also checked calendars and made sure each mentor could make it to a dinner at my place after the summer was over.

The mentors did different things. A few took Jordan camping, and another took him to work. My friend Chuck, who is a police chaplain, took him for a ride in a cruiser and, rumor has it, locked him up in a jail cell. My dad, who immigrated to Canada in 1959 as a teenager, took him through southwestern Ontario and showed him all the places he used to work as a young man trying to make his way in a new country.

When the summer wrapped up, we gathered at our place. It was a great feast. We barbecued some steak, drank Coke, ate ice cream, and ensured there wasn't a salad in sight. It was, after all, a man's meal.

Jordan had kept a journal over the summer, and after dinner he spent some time telling each man what impacted him the most during their days together. Jordan presented each of the men with a Bible with the man's name inscribed on the cover. Each of the mentors then took a few minutes to make some remarks about Jordan and also reflected on some of the gifts they saw at work in his life.

After the men finished, we all gathered around Jordan and laid our hands on him. I read Deuteronomy 6:4–8 and spoke a few words into my son's life, and then we prayed together. Each man took his turn, and Jordan prayed as well. To say it was a powerful moment is an understatement.

As we were wrapping up that night, there wasn't a dry eye in the place. So many of the guys there that night said, "I wish someone had done that for me when I was thirteen." Five years later, I'm still amazed at the power that experience carried.

Just a few months ago, we completed the mentoring process for my younger son, Sam. He had some incredible moments with his mentors last summer, but what struck me at the celebration dinner was how much the experience had impacted the mentors themselves. In fact, the time together was so meaningful for the mentors that over dinner, John (a former pro football player) said that he'd like to gather every year with the guys (and with Sam) for a dinner, if that was okay with Sam. We're officially planning it for next year.

A wider circle has incredible benefits that run in more directions than we might suspect. It became obvious to me as a pastor that other adults could and should have significant relationships with my kids. Understanding the impact some of those mentors had in my sons' lives inspired me to work toward a ministry style that would put weekly mentors in the lives of kids and students.

About a year after Jordan's mentoring year I told the story during a message at the church I lead. People were moved, and numerous people indicated they were going to implement some type of mentoring plan with their son or daughter.

As people filed out, a single mom came to talk to me. I'll never forget Laura's words: "Carey, I love how you had the opportunity to do that with Jordan, and I'm sure it was a great experience, but you're a pastor and you're a guy. You're well-connected. You have men in your life and people around you who you can call on. I'm a single mom. I don't have those connections. Who's going to be there for my son, Aaron?"

That was a reminder of how important it is for the church and parents to partner. The reason it is important to connect with a faith community is that many are designed to encourage leaders who will actually spend time mentoring and coaching kids from all kinds of families.

Heather Zempel speaks firsthand of the impact of this kind of environment. As the minister who leads programs for spiritual growth at National Community Church in Washington DC, Heather points out the difference between a travel agent and a tour guide. A travel agent sits behind a desk and makes arrangements and gives directions. A tour guide walks along with the traveler, answering questions and prompting conversation along the way. As we widen our children's and teenagers' circles to include more tour guides and fewer travel agents, the influence of others will foster lifelong effects.[6]

Next Steps

Look for a church that values community.

Think about it as a parent. Isn't it true if you go back to your story, there is a short list of people who influenced your faith or character? If you could go back and redo your relationships as an adult, you would probably add more of some people in your life and take away some others. People influence us. Most of us can remember people who showed up at the right time, who became a needed voice to give us direction.

What if you could find a ministry or church where your son or daughter could begin developing a sense of community? A community where authentic relationships develop, relationships not only between peers but also with adult leaders. Where trust gets built and healthy friendships form. Your children need someone else to believe in them. They need a place to belong, besides home. The goal is for you to pursue strategic relationships so another adult voice will be speaking into your son's or daughter's life, saying the kinds of things you would try to say as a parent.

The goal is for you to pursue strategic relationships so another adult voice will be speaking into your son's or daughter's life, saying the kinds of things you would try to say as a parent.

Michael Ungar, a social work researcher, offers a powerful metaphor in the book *The We Generation: Raising Socially Responsible Kids*. When parents are not available, "our kids can call for roadside service to get a boost when their emotional batteries go dead." In these times, "other adults can play the roles of mirrors and mentors. Mirrors are people who reflect back to our children their importance. Mentors show our children how to be their best."[7]

A growing number of churches are establishing ministries that prioritize the idea of building community. Even if they have larger group gatherings and other programs, they have a goal to put consistent, trusted adults in the lives of kids and teenagers. One of the most effective ways to build community is through a small group with leaders who get to know the kids and their parents.

Small groups are just what their name implies: a gathering of twelve or fewer who meet together in a group. A small group is typically not led by a traditional teacher but by a leader whose primary task is to build relationships with the kids he or she leads. As kids move into middle and high school, having the same leader in their lives for multiple years can be even more beneficial. The goal is to develop a graduated system where your son or daughter would have consistent leaders with whom they can develop trusted relationships.

Work with other leaders to find opportunities for your kids to serve.

Did you know there is something more important than getting your kids to simply go to church on Sunday mornings? By helping them find opportunities to serve others, you'll encourage them to *be* the church instead of just going to church.

It is too easy for us to find a false sense of security in the notion that our children are growing because they attend something. When we started our churches, we both adopted systems where high school students served on Sunday mornings and had their own small-group time in the afternoon. These students were given several options to serve the church during the morning time, from teaching younger children to working on technical teams to greeting visitors at the door.

Several parents became concerned when we moved teenagers out of Sunday morning classes to this Sunday afternoon group model. They had been programmed, like most parents, to believe that the faith development of their teenagers could happen only in a Sunday morning Sunday school class. No wonder so many of our students graduate from high school and drop out of church. They were never given the opportunity to be the church while they were growing up in church. When parents and leaders work together to encourage students in ministry, a stronger faith is forged.

I (Reggie) told you earlier about how my friend Kevin was a life-changing influence as my son's small-group leader. Kevin tells about how his own son, Brock, has embraced the opportunity to serve. As a high school junior, Brock leads a small group of third-grade boys on Sunday morning. How influential is a high school junior for eight-year-olds? Think high school superhero. Kevin recently saw those third graders show up at Brock's varsity basketball game. They were Brock's biggest fans, not just because he swished a three-pointer, but because he was making a difference in the lives of

Don't underestimate what serving inside the church, in your community, and even globally can do to the heart of your son or daughter.

these younger kids. So if you are Brock's parent, what do you think is more important? That he's sitting in a class, or that Brock's having an experience that is transforming his faith and character?

Don't underestimate what serving inside the church, in your community, and even globally can do to the heart of your son or daughter. We even know some parents and leaders who strive to make sure their teenagers are involved in at least one overseas mission effort before they graduate. They understand how the experience of personal ministry can affect someone's sense of purpose. It is not enough to tell children they are significant. Most of our children will never really believe they are significant until we give them something significant to do.

Search for mentors in your community.

Maybe you don't live near a church that has the kind of ministry we describe. If that's the case, whom do you know within your relational network who could be part of a wider circle? Maybe you have a friend, neighbor, grandparent, or colleague who could be a positive spiritual and moral voice in the life of your son or daughter? If so, why not begin a conversation with that person about a mentoring relationship with your child?

Whatever it takes, as parents we need to become more intentional about widening the circle. If we want to parent beyond our capacity, then we have to tap into the capacity of the faith community around us. Don't forget the color orange. It reminds you that your parenting is not enough. You need to tap into the influence of others. This is a very important value for you to embrace as a mom or dad. Even though it doesn't seem important when children are young, it's more important than it feels. Establishing the principle of community early in their lives can potentially prevent a lot of unnecessary strife later.

When you widen the circle, the goal is to have other trusted adults in the lives of children *before* they need them so they will be there *when* they need them.

When you widen the circle, the goal is to have other trusted adults in the lives of children *before* they need them so they will be there *when* they need them.

Moses passed these values along to the entire community because he knew it would take multiple influences to guard the faith of a generation.

God never intended life to be lived in isolation, and what's true of individuals is also true of families. We have been called to live as part of a much wider circle and God-engineered community to help all of us parent beyond our capacity.

Widen the Circle

DISCUSSION QUESTIONS

Continue the Conversation

Key question: *How am I connecting my child to a wider circle of influence?*

1. When you were young, was there another adult in your life (besides your parents) who gave you good advice and invested in you in a positive way? What impact did this relationship have on you?

2. Many of you did not have another adult who invested in your early years. How might your teenage years have looked different if another adult had been pouring into your life? What knowledge or values do you wish someone had instilled in you as a teenager?

3. How many trusted adults are speaking into your child or teenager's life? What fears and hopes do you have about other leaders being involved in your child or teenager's life?

4. Why does it often feel like you are flying solo as you raise your kids? What next steps could you take, or what places could

you look to widen the circle for your family? How could you and your children begin to experience deeper community?

5. How does the right kind of community create a healthy environment for you to grow as an individual? Specifically, how do you see community being a benefit to your kids?

If you attend a church, start talking to your child about what happened in small group. Who are her friends? What's her small group leader's name? What did they talk about or study? Make sure to introduce yourself to your son or daughter's small group leader. Brainstorm with your child ways to get to know the leader better, like going out for ice cream or having the leader over for a family lunch. (If you are not part of a church that offers community to you and your child, we recommend www.OrangeParents.com for churches in your area.)

Read Deuteronomy 5:1.

> *Moses summoned all Israel and said:*

> *Hear, O Israel, the decrees and laws I declare in your hearing today. Learn them and be sure to follow them.*

Read Deuteronomy 6:4.

> *Hear, O Israel: The Lord our God, the Lord is one.*

Read Deuteronomy 6:5–7.

Love the LORD *your God with all your heart and with all your soul and with all your strength. These commandments that I give you today are to be upon your hearts. Impress them on your children.*

Remember when Moses gave this speech, and imagine being gathered with the Israelites for the talk. Imagine hearing that talk as a parent—would it come as good news, or would you feel overwhelmed? Why?

REFLECT: Imagine hearing the message as someone without kids. If you were a mentor or significant voice in the life of someone else's child or teenager, what could you do to develop a stronger relationship with that child? How would you talk to him or her about faith? How would you develop a trusted friendship with the parents?

CHAPTER FOUR

Family Value #2: Imagine the End

Focus your priorities on what matters most.

I (Reggie) remember watching a documentary several years ago called *The Richest Kids in the World*. My second grader became animated when the reporter described a lavish birthday party hosted by an affluent sheikh for his young son. The sheikh had flown his entire family to London for a special celebration where they were privately entertained by the cast of *Teenage Mutant Ninja Turtles*. The price tag of the party was more than one million dollars. I thought about the extravagant lifestyles of billionaire children, and I played a mental game imagining what I would do with that much money.

A jolt of reality brought me back to my world, and I realized I would never be able to give my children that kind of wealth. I'm ashamed to admit that for a few moments I actually felt a degree of resentment, becoming envious of those parents who were able to provide more than I could. Then I realized: *Most parents can't give their children a lavish inheritance, but every parent will leave a personal legacy.*

With the excess that surrounds most of us, a lot of families get sidetracked from what really matters. We become so preoccupied with giving kids an inheritance that we forget the significance of leaving a legacy. Sometimes I just have to be reminded that what I give *to* my children or what I do *for* my children is not as important as what I leave *in* them. Isn't it interesting how "stuff" can distract us from what is really valuable?

> **What I give *to* my children or what I do *for* my children is not as important as what I leave *in* them.**

Too often, parents believe the end goal is to make their kids happy. There are moments when I will buy anything, do anything, and go anywhere if it will just make my kids *happy*.

Parents don't like it when their kids are in a bad mood. Things are just easier when everybody is happy. You are happy when they are happy, so you'll watch a blue dog on television, eat McNuggets, buy pet turtles, listen to the Wiggles, and mortgage your house if their happiness is at stake. You don't want them to be spoiled; you just want them to be happy.

An entire marketing industry is built around the idea that parents want their kids to be happy. The advertisers know that we will sign them up for anything and everything to make sure they are socially adept, experientially rich, and academically well-rounded. We will recruit coaches, tutors, instructors, and mentors to make sure they can dance better, sing clearer, jump farther, throw faster, hit harder, and test higher than other kids.

At some point, parents cross a line. It's hard to tell where the line is because it's not always obvious in the moment, but I do know I have crossed it before. In my pursuit of what I thought would make my kids happy, I threatened what makes them come alive.

Whenever we define a child's happiness as our ultimate goal, we settle for something far less significant than what God has designed for them or what He has designed them for.

Moses offered a vision of a life well lived with one phrase that establishes a frame of reference for everything:

The LORD our God, the LORD is one.[1]

He begins the passage by reminding Israel about the centrality of faith. He says, "Hear, O Israel [meaning, "Listen and don't forget this"]: The LORD our God, the LORD is one." Moses was saying, *Everything I have said and everything I will say hinges on one essential truth that trumps everything: our God is God.* It's all about Him. Everything is really about God. So if we don't start with God, we may end up in the wrong place.

Moses seems to be making the point that *it really doesn't matter what our kids know if they don't know what really matters.* It would be heartbreaking if your children enjoy the benefits and the prosperity of a better lifestyle, live in a land flowing with milk and honey, and become experientially rich but never really know God.

This passage from Deuteronomy 6 is recited frequently in Judaism. It is referred to as the *shema*, and it is a basic credo for the Jewish faith. Faithful Hebrews since the time of Moses have recited the *shema* twice a day, when they first wake up and just before they go to bed. The *shema* "is the password by which one Jew recognizes another in every part of the world."[2] They hang this passage on their doors as a visual reminder of God's role in their daily lives. It is always present, ever ready to help realign the family's value system in the face of distraction. The practice is not designed to add pressure to the roles of parents but to help them keep perspective. *When you remind yourself frequently that God is God, it doesn't cause you to stress more, it causes you to trust more.* Regardless of what is happening at any unpredictable moment, the character of God provides a predictable context for your story.

The power of the *shema* is that it establishes God as the central character of that story connecting every generation, every family, and every individual to God's goodness. When we can trace His infinite love through time and space, through countless genealogies, it gives us a reason to pause in the middle of our chaos and get clarity.

The shift from trusting in God to trusting in stuff is gradual, but when it happens everything hangs in the balance. It was for this reason God met Moses on the mountain, gave him the first commandment, and warned him about the dangers of idolatry. When it comes to the battle for the heart, what is temporary has a way of crowding out what is eternal. Moses is simply saying, *Stay focused. Don't forget who your God is.*

A Gradual Shift

When Moses encouraged the Hebrew nation to remember "the LORD our God is one," he was warning them about the risk of losing their focus and shifting their priorities. Practically speaking, when families intentionally and consistently embrace the value that God is God, they are more able to parent from a single-minded perspective. The more we remember this is really all about God, the easier it is for us to focus our priorities on what matters most.

A clear view of God's character forces us to come to grips with our smallness and His magnitude. As a parent, I am quick to pick up the yardstick that culture hands me and measure success for my children by a superficial standard. Over time I start thinking the most important thing is for them to attend the right college and find the right career. I want my children to marry the right spouses, live in the right neighborhoods, and have the right friends. I expend enormous energy to make sure I instill the right values. These things are all important … but they are not what is *most* important. Imagining the end is about focusing my priorities on what matters most.

Imagining the end is about focusing my priorities on what matters most.

A Tangible Reminder

Every family has an opportunity to create an environment leveraged with the frequent reminder that "the LORD our God is one." The reason this is so important is because of the nature of what is spiritual—it can't be seen, touched, or felt. Therefore whatever can be seen, touched, or felt gets more attention. We must make a conscious effort to remind ourselves that there is a bigger story and that God is at the center of it.

When I was a teenager, someone challenged me to find an object in my daily routine that could serve as a reminder that God loved me. For some reason, I picked an antique clock that had been given to us by the aunt who raised my mom. It sat in our den, just around the corner from my bedroom, chiming every hour and half hour. For several years I had a built-in alarm to God's faithfulness and presence.

I would hear it when …

> … I woke up in the morning.
> … I had an argument with my parents.
> … I was stressed about school.
> … I was watching TV.
> … I came in from a date.
> … I couldn't sleep at night.

Day after day, it just kept chiming, reminding me of something bigger. Whenever the immediate details of life distracted me, the old clock would give me a cue. It would nudge me back on the right mental track and steer my thinking in the direction of what was eternal. If I became too absorbed with my own problems, started throwing a pity party, or was tempted to think the world should revolve around me, it would sound at a strategic moment.

When Moses stood before the people that day, he was ringing a bell. He was showing us how important it is to recalibrate the heart and give it something to focus on. As a leader, he was modeling to every parent the need to constantly guide

Moses knew that keeping the Hebrew family's focus on God would affirm its identity and shape its destiny.

those they love back to what is core, to what is most valuable. Moses knew that keeping the Hebrew family's focus on God would affirm its identity and shape its destiny.

I have learned that some things are beyond my capacity. As a father of almost-grown children, I have lived through several stages of parenting. I remember walking into my office one day and looking at the rows of books I had collected on family issues. One of my daughters had been through an extremely difficult situation, and I was panicked and frustrated. As I grabbed books off the shelf, I recall saying out loud, "The problem I'm dealing with right now is not in any of these books!" That day I was overwhelmed with the kind of uncertainty and fear that sometimes paralyzes parents. The only way I got any clarity was in realizing that my only comfort, my only hope, my only source for direction was God. Sometimes there are no simple solutions, no clear paths of action, no quick fixes. There is just God.

Somewhere along the way I have learned to lean on a principle we refer to as "imagine the end." The fog usually begins to lift when I mentally fast-forward to the final chapter of my children's lives and ask a pointed question: Who do I really want them to become? I know that in the middle of that answer is an understanding of who God is. Then I imagine the end and remember that God is writing His narrative.

When it comes to my children, the most difficult thing I have ever done is admit my limited capacity and trust God to show up and do what only He can do. *Did I mention I have control issues?* Some days I just need to be reminded that my family is part of a bigger story and that God desires to demonstrate His redemptive power through us. That day in my office, it was if God seemed to say,

> I am not trying to make them happy;
> I want them to really live.

> In the middle of their pain,
> I can be a better friend than anyone,
> even you.

> I am the only One who can really
> *love* them unconditionally,
> *forgive* them forever,
> and be a *perfect* Father.

> So maybe you just need to trust Me
> enough so they can see Me.

> Besides …
> with all of your issues,
> I think it's probably better
> for them to trust Me more
> than they trust you.

> Isn't it more important for them
> to love Me more
> than they love you?

I can heal their hearts;
you can't.
I can give them eternal life;
you can't.
I am God;
you're not.

You Can't Compete with God

As strange as it sounds, I think I sometimes make the mistake of trying to compete with God. Instead of pointing to Him, I try to be the hero. There is a key difference between being an influencer or leader in my kids' lives and trying to be everything to them. Wise parents will strive to make sure they are not trying to

> **When I imagine the end, it enables me to distinguish more clearly between what matters and what matters *most*.**

become a substitute for God. I am learning how important it is to fast-forward to who I want them to become. When I imagine the end, it enables me to distinguish more clearly between what matters and what matters *most*. And as much as I want my relationship with my children to be everything it should be, it's much more important that they are pursuing a right relationship with God.

Most parents feel this responsibility intuitively. If there is even a remote possibility that God actually exists, it only makes logical sense that we would make pursuing a relationship with

Him the highest priority of our life. And if God really created our children and desires to have a relationship with them, then pointing them in His direction should be one of our highest callings. Even parents who struggle with what they believe about God have a sense that they should steer their children to pursue spiritual things. Here is an interesting fact: According to a study by Barna Research Group, 85 percent of parents believe they are primarily responsible for our children's spiritual development. Ninety-six percent of us feel primarily responsible for our children's moral development.[3]

If you read what most Christian parenting books tell you about your role, it can be a little unnerving. They seem to suggest that you are basically responsible for two things in your kids' lives:

(1) You are supposed to be the best picture of God they can tangibly see.
(2) You are supposed to lead your kids to be as much like God as they can be.

Is it just me, or does that seems like a little too much pressure? The idea that their image and perception of God is determined by how I parent begins to create serious doubts in my mind about my capacity to do the job. Add to it the pressure of getting my kids to become godly, and I am panicked.

I actually remember trying to have a conversation about this with my youngest daughter, Rebekah, when she was in the fifth grade. I think I was trying to establish a disclaimer so I would feel better about my role. I remember saying to her, "You know I just get nervous sometimes because I am supposed to be the closest example to you of what God, your heavenly Father, is like." It got kind of quiet in the car, and she said, "Dad, you don't need to worry about that. I don't think I will ever get the two of you mixed up. You're definitely not God."

The problem is this: A lot of parents are not sure what to do or where to begin when it comes to developing faith and character in the hearts of their children. Most of us who have grown up in churches have heard that parents are supposed to lead their children spiritually. And if we are honest, we don't always feel spiritual, and we are not sure we know how to lead.

Think about the term *spiritual leader* for a moment. Consider what that phrase actually means. We often use passed-down phrases while never stopping to ask what exactly they mean. If you were to write a clear definition of *spiritual leadership*, what would it be? As parents, we often feel intimidated by terms like this. As a result we are not sure it's something we can do. Maybe it's time to redefine spiritual leadership in terms that are practical and possible.

Several years ago, I was invited to a meeting by the leaders of a national ministry to brainstorm ideas for partnering with parents. When the meeting started, the facilitator walked to the whiteboard and wrote 2 Timothy 3:17 on it: "So that the man of God may be thoroughly equipped for every good work." He took his marker and wrote the words "THOROUGHLY EQUIPPED MAN OF GOD" on the board in huge letters. Then he said that if we could get every man in our country to become a "thoroughly equipped man of God," we'd solve the family crisis in America.

As the facilitator continued explaining that our group was to come up with ideas to help men become the standard-bearers of that passage, I started getting uneasy. The letters on the board seemed overwhelming. I felt like they were just staring at me. It seemed like he just kept repeating them over and over. I remember thinking at some point, *I don't believe I can recall my wife ever using the words "thoroughly equipped," "man of God," and my name in the same sentence. I have middle-schoolers. By the time I become a "thoroughly equipped man of God," they'll be married with children of their own. I'm not sure I can ever be whatever that is, and I am not even sure what it means.*

I think this all comes back to the issue of personal capacity. Do you ever listen to experts talk about what you should be as a parent and think, "I'm just not qualified"? Several years ago we decided to write down a definition of *spiritual leadership* that would be a practical, possible guide for parents:

> Spiritual leadership means parents assume the primary responsibility to help their kids take the next step in their pursuit of a relationship with God.

We sometimes get overwhelmed because we look too far ahead when our focus should really be on the next step. Our involvement is no different from what you would do to help children with schoolwork or to care for them when they are sick. No parent is going to say, "I can't help you with your homework. I didn't get an education degree," or, "I can't make sure you take your medicine. I'm not qualified to be a doctor." You are responsible to do what you can to promote their education and protect their health.

It doesn't mean we have to understand everything there is to understand about God. It doesn't mean we have to have a degree in Bible. It doesn't even mean we have to be as "spiritual" as we think leaders in the church may be. Spiritual leadership involves one of the levers we discussed in the last chapter. It simply implies that we are leveraging our relationships as parents to help our kids keep moving in their relationship with God.

My dad and I are very different. He was born in the Great Depression, and his dad farmed cotton. Dad joined the Air Force when he was a teenager to get away from some things.

He's reserved. I'm emotional.

He uses a PC. I use a Mac.

He doesn't say a lot. I talk too much.

He's a saver. I'm a spender.

He can fix or build anything. I had a mechanical bypass.

He's a little stubborn, strong-willed, and opinionated. I'm …

well, we are different in *most* ways.

I remember sitting down a few years ago and pondering how my dad moved the spiritual lever in my life and influenced my faith. I was only a year old when he and Mom decided to move us away from all our relatives to Memphis.

During that time, a group of Christian couples became friends with my parents, and Mom and Dad rediscovered church. I can remember growing up in Sunday School and hanging out with those Christian families every Sunday night after church, long before anyone told us about the importance of being in a "group."

They modeled an authentic and relational faith to our family and encouraged my parents in their spiritual journeys.

I watched my dad get ordained as a deacon in our church when I was eight. The only other time I ever saw him cry was when his own father died. I was baptized that same year, and Dad started auditing a few Bible college classes just to learn more. As the years passed, he would pass along tapes from his professors and let me listen to what they said about the existence of God and a host of other issues I had questions about as a teenager.

I remember vividly a season in my life when I was wrestling with some private thoughts and temptations. It was one of those times when I really didn't know anyone I could trust with my questions. One night he "accidently" left a cassette tape called "The Cry of an Unhappy Christian" on the desk in my room. The message contained a life-changing truth for me that helped me understand the concept of God's grace at an early age.

When I decided I wanted to start a ministry working with teenagers, Dad sold a number of things from the house, including our pool table, to buy audio equipment to use when I traveled. I bet you are thinking my dad was some kind of saint, but the funny thing is I never thought of him that way. We never had long intimate conversations about his relationship with God. We never did a Bible study together or had a spiritual rite of passage ceremony. I don't think my dad would qualify himself as "a thoroughly equipped man of God." He struggled like most parents. But in his own way, my father figured out how to leverage his influence to point me toward a relationship with God.

Although a number of men have made an impact in my faith, his influence was different. Why? He was my dad. He had a sense that God was important for our family and that we all needed to keep pursuing something that was spiritual and eternal.

I think my parents practiced the principle of imagining the end without even realizing it. God was a priority in our home. They also widened the circle of influences in my life when they built healthy friendships with other parents and leaders in the faith community. A number of those adults became important voices in my life.

You may be wondering, "But what exactly does that mean I am supposed to do as a parent? How do I influence my son or daughter to take the next step spiritually?" We are not going to give you a checklist. Our collective experience suggests it so unique and different for every child that it simply involves using whatever limited capacity you have to connect your family to God's unlimited capacity.

In *ScreamFree Parenting*, Hal Runkel writes,

> You need to create a space for your child to develop a relationship with God on his own terms. Does this mean you do nothing? Of course not. You actively create faith discussions throughout your child's development. You introduce him to the faith tradition that's led you thus far, and, above all, you live in a way that reflects the highest values of that faith…. The ultimate goal of parenting is to launch our children into an adulthood where they are self-directed, decisive, and responsible people.[4]

We began this conversation by talking about legacy, the inheritance of faith that each parent can pass on to the next generation. My dad and mom could never have given me a billionaire birthday any more than Debbie and I could have done that for our kids, but my parents built in me something far more valuable and lasting. They gave me the encouragement and room to pursue a faith that was my own.

Imagine the End

DISCUSSION QUESTIONS

Continue the Conversation

Key Question: *Who do I want my child to become?*

1. Fast-forward to some of the big moments in your children's future: getting a diploma, getting a first job, getting married. Picture the scene in your mind. Who is there to celebrate? How are your children participating in this big moment? What have they done to get there? What is happening in the relationships closest to them? What does your relationship with them look like?

2. When you think back on the past month, where did you spend most of your time as a parent? What were you dealing with on a regular basis? Handling urgent things (like sleep, nutrition, discipline) often means that significant personal development (like spiritual growth, wise decision-making skills, and morality) never makes it to the top of the priority list. How do you handle this tension in your home?

3. What do you think God is most concerned about: what you do, what you acquire, or who you become?

4. How does society help or hurt you as you try to focus on the most important things in life? How does Deuteronomy 6 help you stay focused?

5. Earlier in this chapter, I (Reggie) wrote about a clock in my house that reminded me to focus on God every time I heard it chime. What tangible object does your family encounter every day that could serve as the same kind of reminder?

Challenge

Ask God to help you gain a clear picture of who you want your children to become as they grow to become adults.

- What does their relationship with God look like?
- How would you describe their character?
- What would those who are close to them say about them?

Ask God to help you focus more on who your children are becoming than what they are doing at any given moment. Watch how your attitude, your perspective, and your priorities begin to change as you parent your children with the end in mind.

CHAPTER FIVE

Family Value #3: Fight for the Heart

Communicate in a style that gives the relationship value.

I (Carey) remember one morning when my older son was thirteen and my younger son was around nine. My wife was gone for the day, so it was my turn to cook breakfast. About the only thing I know how to make is pancakes, so I was at the counter mixing flour and eggs and whatever else needs to be combined to make pancakes. Even though cooking is not my thing, it was the best part of the morning.

Both my sons were in a mood that day. They are generally great kids, but neither of them was particularly kind, cooperative, or helpful that morning.

I couldn't get them to do what I wanted them to do. I pulled out all of my parenting tricks. Reasoning. Appeals to the greater good. Guilt. Veiled threats. Direct threats. Exasperation. Nothing worked that day.

Finally I looked at my older son, Jordan, and said in a rather loud voice, "Go sit on the time-out chair."

I realize that was a crazy thing to say to a thirteen-year-old. I hadn't used the time-out chair on him in years, but it was my last-ditch effort at trying not to completely lose my mind.

Jordan looked back at me defiantly and said, "You can't make me sit on the time-out chair. I'm thirteen years old!"

That about did it.

I was completely out of parenting tricks with absolutely nothing intelligent, spiritual, or appropriate left to say. I told him I was bigger than he was, that I was his father, and that if I wanted to make a thirteen-year-old sit on the time-out chair, I could, so he had better sit down right now.

I think more out of pity or fear than obedience, he sat on the chair. Embarrassed. At thirteen. On the time-out chair.

Sometimes it is easy to forget that you can win the argument and force the right behavior but lose the heart in the process.

Like a lot of dads, I get wound up when my authority is challenged. It's in me as a man to go head-to-head and fight to win the argument, to crush the rebellion, and to prove that I am in charge. Sometimes it is easy to forget that you can win the argument and force the right behavior but lose the heart in the process.

Over those pancakes, I realized the importance of fighting for the heart.

In so many ways, I'm grateful for that insight and that moment.

I am a graduate of law school (my first training), and I've always loved rules (I'm not claiming I always follow them, just that I like them). Five years ago, had you asked me, I still might have said that obedience has greater value than love.

When Reggie and I started working together on parenting issues, my oldest son was entering his teen years. As we began to develop these materials, I saw how much I would need to become a student of what we were writing.

I could see my default parenting style heading for a fight that was ultimately unwinnable. In our home of four people, we have two lawyers (my wife and I) and three firstborns. If you thought there might be strong opinions in our home, you would be correct. But what became clearer to me as my kids grew older was that winning an argument actually isn't winning. A fifteen-year-old won't respond to a style of interaction to which he or she responded at age five. Your control naturally diminishes as a child becomes a teenager and then an adult. Seeing clearly the priority of love and communicating in a way that gives the relationship value has helped me tremendously as a father and husband.

Every family fights, but there is a world of difference between when you fight *with* someone and when you fight *for* someone. When you fight with someone, you want to win. When you fight for someone, you want that person to win. When you fight with people, walls are built up. When you fight for people, walls come down. When you fight with people, relationships are jeopardized. When you fight for people, relationships are prioritized.

I am so thankful as a husband, as a dad, and as a person that I have seen the value of fighting for the heart. For me, I believe it came just in time.

For the people of God, Moses' discourse in Deuteronomy 6 also came just in time.

Moses had spent his entire life of leadership trying to get the people of Israel to obey. Several stories in the Old Testament tell of how he battled with their wills. But when we come back to Deuteronomy 6, Moses seems to approach the laws of God with a different perspective, that of a more seasoned leader.

In this chapter, Moses challenges the entire Hebrew nation as these wanderers are about to move into Canaan. He recounts their story over the previous forty years and then reminds them of their covenant with God. At a pivotal moment, he reestablishes the cornerstone principle of the nation when he says, "Hear O Israel: The LORD our God, the LORD is one."[1]

Up until this point, there had not been anything too novel about his words. It had been a healthy review of God's activity through the years and the commandments He had given them. Then Moses says something that grips their attention, something that is recorded for the first time in Scripture, something Jesus Himself would repeat and amplify fifteen hundred years later.

> *Love the LORD your God with all your heart and with*
> *all your soul and with all your strength.*[2]

Forty years earlier, Moses stepped off Mount Sinai with the commandments God wanted Moses to deliver to His people. Tucked away in the middle of those commandments was a short reference so brief in comparison to the rest of the law that it almost went unnoticed.

In Exodus 20, after God had explained His commandment

against worshipping other gods or idols, He touched on the core issue that separates a system of religion from a relational faith. In verse 6, God says He will show His love "to a thousand [generations] of those who love me and keep my commandments." The reference seems almost insignificant in the body of text, but it makes an important connection between love and obedience.

Prior to this passage there are few, if any, references in the Old Testament that point to a person's expressed love for God or to the relationship of that love to His commandments. There are passages about God loving people and about human love for one another, but not a person's love for God.

Most of the text until this point suggests the need for people to worship, respect, and fear God. That's why the words Moses speaks in Deuteronomy 6 are so pivotal for Hebrew culture. He has been on the mountain with God, lived Israel's story, and has a frame of reference like no one else.

In one sentence he connects the dots to give them an even better understanding of the big picture. What he says in this one phrase changes the conversations that the Jewish people will have for thousands of years. He explains the missing link that so often occurs when we allow our faith to become a system of rules.

> The only thing that separates a living faith
> from a ritualistic orthodoxy
> is one word,
> one idea,
> one compelling force:
> Love.

Moses clearly connects the idea of obeying God's commandments to the issue of love, then takes the concept of loving God to a much deeper level. He puts a cornerstone in place that Jesus will later use to build an entire kingdom. Over the next several chapters Moses will restate this command more than a dozen times.

> Love the LORD your God with all your heart and with
> all your soul and with all your strength.

Moses is fighting for something that is more important than lifestyle or practice. He is fighting for the hearts of those who will follow.

If you want to pass on a legacy to the next generation, it has to be transferred relationally. Anytime you pass down rules, practices, or truths outside of the context of a genuine, compelling love, you establish an empty religion. You promote

If you want to pass on a legacy to the next generation, it has to be transferred relationally.

an orthodoxy that will ultimately die, become abusive, or even incite rebellion. Moses was drawing a circle around the entire faith of his people, and it centers on loving God.

A New Rule

As the Israelites approach the Promised Land, Moses reminds them of this key truth once again. Don't forget the context of Moses' speech: The Israelites' past was colliding with their future. Everything had been leading up to this moment. It wasn't just that Moses was setting them up for what he wanted to say that day. God had been setting them up for decades for what He wanted to seal in their hearts forever.

What Moses does in his presentation is genius. In one hand, he holds the chapter that outlined their history up to this point, reminding them of their disobedience and of God's faithfulness. In the other hand, he holds a new chapter that describes the reality of Canaan. The contrast is amazing: There *was* the wilderness, and *now* there is Canaan. There *were* the inconsistencies of a nation's faith, and *now* there is the ultimate demonstration of God's faithfulness.

Moses is saying, *God is doing what He promised: You are about to taste the honey and take a walk on the beach. It's settled now! God did what He has been saying He would do.* As Moses stands there, he connects the past chapters of their heritage to their future with that one pivotal statement: "Love the LORD your God with all your heart and with all your soul and with all your strength."

Why now? How is this relevant to the legacy? They are about to realize the blessings of Canaan—what does that have to do with enduring in faith and loving God? Besides, how can you *command* people to love?

Moses was forthright: *From now on everything should be different. Based on what you have seen and what you know now, you should stop thinking of God only as someone you fear, but as someone you can love. What is about to happen should settle what you believe about the character of God forever. God keeps His promises. God can be trusted with your heart, your soul, and your strength. He is giving you Canaan not because you deserve it, not because of who you are, but because He is God. He has no reason to do what He is doing for you except that He wants to make a lasting impression on you about His nature.*

Your story is about to transition to a new chapter. From now on, the story will be told differently. It will have a climax it never had before, a resolution that will establish a different frame of reference. From this point on you should transition from a people who simply obey rules to a people who pursue a love relationship with their Creator God. And remember that there is a generation following you and watching your response to your God.

Moses is establishing a new commandment that supersedes all commandments. This new rule implies that there is something more important than the rules. It elevates the significance of a relationship with God above everything else, indicating that our motive for obedience should mature beyond fear or reverence. *Moses was warning the people about the danger of passing down rules without the context of a loving relationship.*

This new rule implies that there is something more important than the rules.

This is so relevant for parents. Most parents buy into the idea that what is most important is to pass down the rules and the reasons for the rules. If they simply explain *why* they have the rule, then it will result in a different response and behavior from their children, right? If it makes sense, if it's logical, then they will behave. If Webster's dictionary, the Bible, and Dr. Phil all agree, then certainly there should be a consensus in the home.

Truthfully, though, I don't recall a time when I gave such a wonderful explanation of the rules that my children agreed and said in unison, "Oh, now we understand, Father! You have explained it so well. We will do exactly what you say." The problem with rules and reasons is that you can debate them—but you can't debate a trusted relationship. Unfortunately, most of us parents are better skilled at fighting to win the argument than we are at fighting to win the heart.

It's not that parents shouldn't give answers when kids ask, "Why?" It's just that the answers never carry more weight than a healthy relationship. One of the most powerful things a parent can do is learn to communicate in a style that values the relationship.

> **One of the most powerful things a parent can do is learn to communicate in a style that values the relationship.**

Thousands of years ago, parents faced the same family issues that we do today. Moses told the Hebrew families there would come a day when their kids would question the rules. In Deuteronomy 6:20, he says, "In the future, when your son asks you, 'What is the meaning of the stipulations, decrees and laws the LORD our God has commanded you?'" …

Now stop for just a second.

If you're a parent, does that resemble any of your conversations with your kids? I'm not sure about the age of the son in this verse, but let's say he was somewhere around thirteen years old. I can imagine a Jewish parent sitting with Moses in therapy saying, "I don't know what went wrong. I let him have the reins to the camel. He has access to the oasis in the backyard. He had his own private tent. Now he's complaining about the rules. He doesn't want to show up for any of the feast days, and he's asking questions about Passover. What I am supposed to do?"

There were many times in my (Reggie's) home when one of my kids would ask "Why?" and I would overreact. I would pull out the whiteboard and draw a line down the middle and begin, "On this side of the line is what will happen if you do what is wrong, and on the other side are the benefits of doing what is right. As your father, I have thirty years of experience, plus your mother and God agree with me on this. Besides, if you don't do this, you'll be grounded for a month. Any questions?"

Moses gives the people interesting advice in this situation. He advises them that whenever the son asks the meaning of the stipulations and the laws, "tell him: 'We were slaves of Pharaoh in Egypt [Translated: "Son, you think you feel like a slave because of these rules? You have no idea. Let me tell you what real slavery is like."], but the LORD brought us out of Egypt with a mighty hand. Before our eyes the LORD sent miraculous signs and wonders— great and terrible—upon Egypt and Pharaoh and his whole household. But he brought us out from there to bring us in and give us the land that he promised on oath to our forefathers. The LORD commanded us to obey all these decrees and to fear the LORD our God, so that we might always prosper and be kept alive, as is the case today.'"[3]

Moses' response doesn't really sound like an answer to the child's question. It sounds more like he's telling a story about how great God has been. Moses is not giving a lot of practical reasons here except for the fact that God can be trusted.

Moses wanted future generations to see how they were personally linked to that bigger story, how they fit into a master plan.

He wants children to understand they are part of a bigger story in which God is actively involved and has proven how much He loves them since the beginning of time.

Moses wanted future generations to see how they were personally linked to that bigger story, how they fit into a master plan, and how they were connected to a relationship with their Creator. Instead of encouraging parents to assume the role of attorneys who build a logical case for why the law should be followed, Moses prompted them to focus on the character of the Lawgiver.

The most important way you fight for the heart is to build a relationship that is trustworthy. This is a crucial parenting principle modeled in God's relationship with the children of Israel. The story of the Hebrew race is a story that documents the actions of a Father who is unchanging in His devotion. The main point of the epic is that God can *always* be trusted.

He miraculously delivered the Israelites from slavery.

He continued loving them when they ignored His instructions.

He never stopped leading them throughout their wilderness experience.

He refused to disown them despite their skeptical and rebellious behavior.

The point that echoes through time and generations is that God will always fight for the hearts of the people He loves. That's why Moses can stand at the crossroads of generations and say, *You can give God your heart and soul. You should love Him with everything, because you can trust Him forever.*

The immaturity and inconsistency of Israel's behavior actually became an effective backdrop to highlight God's faithfulness. In a similar way, the unpredictable and rebellious actions of children provide an opportunity for parents to demonstrate a consistent message.

Parents need to understand the significance of this principle as they attempt to fight for the hearts of their children. Too often, parents think their primary goal is to get their children to follow the rules. One of the greatest gifts parents can give to their children is simply to prove that parents can be trusted over the long haul. *During the formative and teenage years, it is actually more essential for the parents to earn trust with the child than it is for the child to earn trust with the parents.*

Chap Clark has been a speaker at our Orange Conference, and he offers some strong insights about creating a healthy structure for adolescents: "[Moms and dads] need to see their parental role as a marathon, recognizing that building a relationship in which their child trusts them is even more important than whether they can trust their child regarding the immediate issues of the day."[4]

I (Reggie) wish someone had told me that when I started out as a parent. Although it may seem intuitive, intentionality is required for consistency. It's ironic that sometimes my reaction to what I see as broken trust on their part can affect their confidence in me. The truth is that their trust in me is affected when I …

> … discipline in anger.
> … use words that communicate rejection.
> … ignore their voices.
> … don't try to understand who they really are.
> … break my core promises.
> … take things too personally.

I have four children: a boy and three girls. One of the clearest lessons I learned about family was from my youngest, Rebekah, when she was in the seventh grade. As the youngest, she has developed some pretty amazing verbal skills to survive her older siblings.

One afternoon we were in her room having a conversation—a rather loud one. It was one of those "you're thirteen and you will do what I say and I am your father and you have to listen to me and that's just the way it is" kind of moments.

That's when it happened. She took a verbal shot at me that totally caught me off guard. It hit me so hard I actually heard myself catch my breath. I never dreamed one of my children would ever say what she said to me in that moment. (In all fairness to her, she had been trying to tell me something that had been going on, and I had not been paying attention. So it was really an attempt on her part to get me to listen.)

I was so shocked. I had no comeback. It was so personal that I was extremely hurt. I did the only thing I could think to do at that moment. I left. I walked out of the room, down the stairs, through the den, and into the garage. I got in my car and drove off. Have I already said that I was really upset, and very, very personally offended?

I was driving down the road, feeling betrayed. About fifteen minutes into the drive, my mobile phone rang. It was Rebekah.

When I answered, she said, "Dad, I'm sorry. You know I really didn't mean what I said." Then she said, "But why did you leave? Why did you walk out? I need to know that our relationship is worth fighting for." It was one of those moments where the parent becomes the child.

I can't really prove this because I don't have any statistical information to back it up, but I think Rebekah verbalized what a lot of teenagers think at some point. She was merely suggesting that she needed to know she could trust me to never stop fighting for our relationship.

I have talked with college-aged girls whose fathers have stopped fighting for their relationships with their daughters because they lost the battle for their marriages. I have talked to sons who have strained relationships with parents because they became disengaged relationally after conflicts in high school.

As parents we make a drastic mistake if we stop fighting, yielding to the misconception that maybe our kids don't need a relationship with us. Some of you have gravitated away from making those relationships a priority because it's just too hard.

It's easier to focus on the child's need to earn trust than to actively pursue my need to build trust as a parent. We get so absorbed with molding them into what they should be that we forget our need to develop consistency in how we respond to them.

How trustworthy we are as parents is much more important for their growth than how trustworthy they are.

It takes a long time as a parent to realize the negative impact when any degree of trust is breached with our kids. How trustworthy we are as parents is much more important for their growth than how trustworthy they are.

In our personal interviews with hundreds of teenagers and

college students, the wounds that go deepest are those connected to the issue of trust. When we fight for the hearts of our children, we establish a lifestyle of proving we can be trusted. This doesn't mean we always make the right decisions, have the best rules, or can explain the perfect reasons. When it comes to our capacity, it doesn't mean that we never get tired of the countless issues or struggles related to parenting. It simply means we never stop fighting for our relationship with each other.

Richard Halverson, chaplain of the U.S. Senate from 1981 until 1994, said it this way: "If you're going to fight … fight for the relationship, not against it."[5]

Parents and leaders need to agree that family and church should be about more than rules. It's a place where trusted relationships are built, where every member of the family can experience a different quality of love.

Within the community of faith that he was addressing, Moses knew a secret about obedience—it starts when you really believe that God can be trusted. He knew that if the generation of parents and leaders he was speaking to would choose to love God with all their hearts and souls, it would show up in their

Your ability, your strength, your desire to love your children the right way starts with learning how to love God the right way.

personal lifestyles and be contagious in their children. As a result, those who trusted God would be trusted by the next generation. That is the kind of loving and trusted relationship that fuels the emotional and moral health of a generation.

Maybe Moses understood something else even more important that we should never forget: that our capacity to love our children and family is somehow linked to our love for God. Stated another way, if you want to love your children beyond your capacity, then learn to love God. The point is, God's love is much more powerful and trustworthy than even your love as a parent. Your ability, your strength, your desire to love your children the right way starts with learning how to love God the right way.

Fight for the Heart

DISCUSSION QUESTIONS

Continue the Conversation

Key Question: *How am I fighting for the heart of my child?*

1. Talk about the home you grew up in. What was the approach to rules and discipline in your childhood home?

2. Were rules enforced in the context of a loving relationship? Were the rules sometimes sacrificed for the sake of the relationship, or did relationships become secondary to enforcing the rules? How do you think this has impacted your home, positively or negatively, today?

3. Think back to the last time you fought *with* your kids. Now, think back to the last time you fought *for* them. How did each of those experiences leave you feeling? What are your insights on the value of fighting for your kids rather than with them?

4. Make a list of everyone in your house. Off to the side, write down what you are most likely to fight about with that person. Why do you think these things tend to be hot-button issues for the two of you?

5. How do you think you can work at getting to the root of the issue? In other words, what does each of you really want in the situation? *(Note: What each of you really wants might not be obvious; it might not be the specific thing you are fighting about.)*

6. Make a list of places where some of your best and most honest conversations with your children have occurred. Was it tucking them in bed, driving in the car, playing catch in the yard, or doing a project together?

> *In the movie* Father of the Bride, *there's a great scene with Steve Martin's character (George Banks) and his daughter, Annie. Things have not turned out the way he expected, and the conversation escalates. But then George gets an idea. He and his daughter talk things through on the driveway basketball court, a place where they'd spent many hours through the years building their relationship.*

7. Seek to recreate scenarios like these for natural conversations when neither of you are upset. Talk about these insights with your spouse or another parent so you can encourage each other.

Read Deuteronomy 6:5.

> Love the LORD your God with all your heart and with all your soul and with all your strength.

REFLECT: Why do you think God established love, rather than obedience, as a priority over all things? Is this principle hard for you to relate to in your own relationship with God? Take some time today to pray for every person in your family and your relationship with them.

CHAPTER SIX

Family Value #4: Create a Rhythm

Increase the quantity of quality time you spend together.

Okay, let's recap.

If you are operating from a Better Picture, greener-grass mindset for your family, you are going to run out of steam fast. Keep thinking in terms of a bigger story that your family still has yet to tell, regardless of the past. Remember that in the context of that bigger story, you are not alone as a parent. You are not designed to do this solo, and your children need other influences besides just you. There is a wider circle you can leverage to influence your children beyond your limited capacity. God designed all of us to be a part of a larger community of faith in order to grow in our relationship with him. When parents and leaders of this community work together with the same end in mind and prioritize for what matters most, we can make a greater impact in the heart of a child. When it comes to your relationship with your children, you should fight for their hearts by building an environment in your home of unconditional love and trust. Oh, and here's something else we need to talk about that is related to your capacity—

Time.

It's moving fast.

It's limited.

We will never have more of it than we already have.

So the issue is not how do we get more,

but how do we become more intentional about what we have?

How can we manage our time strategically to parent beyond our capacity?

Every family has a rhythm. You don't have to intend to have one. You don't have to plan one. We all end up with one. You have one. Your family has one. As we go from day to day, we establish and shape a rhythm that in turn shapes our kids. Rhythm is simply how we arrange our time.

If you were to analyze the rhythm at your house, you would soon discover that much of your family life consists of repeated patterns.

If you were to analyze the rhythm at your house, you would soon discover that much of your family life consists of repeated patterns. As much as we resist that thought because we like to think of ourselves as free beings, we actually behave like creatures of habit. If you don't believe that, take a different route home from work, switch places at the dinner table, or change up the side of the bed you sleep on.

That's why we (try to) put newborns on a schedule as soon as possible. It's why we tend to go to the same gas station, because familiar is efficient. It's why we keep a calendar, why we set up family nights, why TV shows lock into a time slot and stay there, why churches don't randomly alter service times and dates (*Hey ... church this week is Thursday at 3 a.m.*), why stores open and close on a schedule, and why we have alarm clocks. Our lives are largely programmed around a rhythm.

Rhythm and structure determine more than we think. I (Carey) remember taking my first class field trip as a dad when Jordan was in kindergarten. We were headed to the zoo, and having only been a dad for a few years, I wasn't sure what a day spent with four- and five-year-olds was going to be like. I was hoping the monkeys would seem civilized and bring a moment of sanity into my day. I really went because I didn't want to be the dad who never showed up at my kids' events.

I walked into the kindergarten classroom and was blown away by Jordan's teacher and class. She actually had them sitting quietly. Then I heard her speak ever so calmly. She laid down the expectations for the day as though she was talking to a graduate class at Harvard.

These children, who mostly didn't know their alphabet, spoke only when spoken to and lined up for the bus like there was an invisible force field aligning their movement. It surprised me that the teacher didn't raise her voice once. They were the best-behaved group of school kids I'd ever seen—and they were fewer than thirty days into their first school experience.

As the kids filed onto the bus, I leaned over to her and said, "You are so fortunate to have a class that's this obedient."

She looked at me and said, "Oh no, *every* class is like this."

My face must have shown my shock. I replied, "No way. They *can't* be all like that."

"Yes, they are," she replied. "It's all about the expectations you establish with them from the outset."

As I reflected on her comments, I began to see how much rhythm factored into how she led classes.

Rhythm sets certain expectations and eliminates others. The rhythm she set up pretty much eliminated confusion from the daily menu. The kids knew when to sit, when to stand, how to show courtesy when asking a question. They knew the schedule, when lunch would come, when reading time happened, and when it was time for naps. (Remember nap time?)

Rhythm in your home actually shapes your family values.

Rhythm in your home actually shapes your family values. Think about it. It establishes what is acceptable and what is not acceptable. The rhythm in your home determines what gets talked about and what doesn't get talked about.

You have a normal flow of conversation. As a family settles into a routine, much of the daily conversation can become transactional: Did you brush your teeth? Is your homework done? What's for dinner? The after-school exchange can easily become, "What happened at school today?" "Nothing." Rhythm can tilt us away from meaningful dialogue or lean us into it.

This is how rhythm establishes value. Things that become part of the daily rhythm are the things our families will come to believe are most important. Rhythm silently but significantly communicates value.

Some parts of life may be conceptually very important to us as parents, but if we never include them in our families' rhythms, our kids will perceive them as having little value. For example, exercise might be important to a parent in principle, but if no one ever plays baseball in the backyard, takes a trip to the park, throws a Frisbee, jumps on a treadmill, or heads to a soccer field or hockey rink, why would the kids come to value exercise? If it's not part of their rhythm, it's not part of their reality.

The Good China

What happens every day in your home defines what normal becomes for your family. It may become normal to go camping every summer. It might become normal to eat turkey at Christmas but have hamburgers on Saturday. Normal might include going to school, spending an hour on homework after school, going to the movies once a month, having friends over every Friday night, and knowing that Dad is passionate about keeping his car in great shape. Parents determine what's normal by the rhythm they establish in their homes.

So—and here's the key question—how normal is God in your home?

I know that sounds like a strange question. Culturally, it *is* a strange question. But as we'll see shortly, God may not have intended it to be that bizarre.

Some of us are just old enough to have still received fine china as a wedding gift. These days, we're wondering why it was a priority, because we never use it.

Our kids don't see it as normal because it rarely comes out of the cabinet. When it does come out, the kids figure someone special must be coming over, everyone's concerned about whether it breaks or not, and we all tend to get a little more uptight.

Consequently, our china set has missed a lot over the life of our family. It missed almost all the conversations we've had over dinner. It missed the laughter, the wrestling after supper, and some hilarious times with the four of us and with friends. It missed all the practical jokes we've played on each other and all the snacks during movies. It missed the arguments, the tears, and the seemingly incurable hiccups. It pretty much missed everything. If you asked my kids if they ever wanted it as an inheritance, they'd likely say no. It just isn't part of anyone's life. (Please don't ask them about our flat-screen TV, though.)

We haven't thrown the china out because it cost a lot of money, and it's important in the sense that valuable possessions are important. It just doesn't see day-to-day life very often.

Some of us grew up with a faith like that.

God was important, but He just didn't come out much in the daily rhythm of life.

Some of you grew up in a home where faith was never talked about. You never went to church on Sunday, and God never came up during the week. It wasn't part of your rhythm at all.

Some of you grew up in a home where God was part of a Sunday rhythm, but like fine china, He never showed up on any other day.

Some of you grew up in a home where God was part of a Sunday rhythm, but like fine china, He never showed up on any other day. You didn't pray at meals. God was never part of a daily dialogue. In fact, you could never figure out how the God of Sunday had any claim on everyday life. It was just a mystery to you. You knew it was important. You believed at some level that God had value. But like the china in your cabinet, God just didn't see much time in your family's life.

Some of you grew up in a decidedly Christian home, and God was part of a rhythm. For some of us, it felt like a bit of an awkward rhythm. A well-meaning and sincere parent would bring out the big Bible after dinner. A passage would be read. And then questions would be asked. I've tried that as a parent, and it's all good until the uncomfortable "no one's answering my questions and can we please just be excused" moment that inevitably follows. It feels so formal, as though it isn't actually connected to everyday life. Somehow faith ends up feeling like a compartment we step into for a moment rather than a conversation that's woven into the fabric of life.

That's the difference between a God who is at the center of the family and one who is put up on the shelf and only taken out for special occasions.

An Everyday Faith

As we meet up with Moses again, we see that the people of Israel were at a point where they were about to transition from one cultural rhythm to another.

They had spent forty years wandering around the desert. It wouldn't be pleasant to wander the desert every day for a generation. But the upside is that people became very dependent on

God for everyday things. You don't feed hundreds of thousands of people in the desert three meals a day without some help from God.

For a generation, they received *daily* reminders about who God was and how *dependent* they were on God for everything. There was the manna they depended on *every day* to eat. There was the cloud of smoke that hovered over them *every day* to lead the way. There was even a pillar of fire that was there *every night* when they went to sleep.

This nomadic people knew a God who was very present in their *everyday* experience.

Remember, self-reliance is a fairly recent phenomenon. There were no fast-food restaurants, no computers, no cell phones, no movie theatres, no televisions, no video games, no concerts, no iTunes, iPods, iPhones, digital photography, jet skis, *Monday Night Football,* indoor plumbing, air-conditioned buildings, or even Starbucks. I mean, they really *needed* God, and He was very obviously present.

But Moses was aware that their current existence would not be their future reality. One translation of what he was saying might go like this: "If you are going to impress these truths in the hearts of your children, you will have to be more deliberate about *creating a rhythm* within your home. In the future, there will be a host of things that will distract you. You will get comfortable. You will grow prosperous. You will get distracted. Life will get

If you are going to impress these truths in the hearts of your children, you will have to be more deliberate about *creating a rhythm* within your home.

busy, and it will be easy to drift away from the importance of having an *everyday* kind of faith."

Moses knew that in Canaan, families would have to be …

> … more conscious about creating a rhythm that transferred an everyday faith.
>
> … more deliberate about establishing visual reminders of God's power and presence.
>
> … more innovative about how and when they told God's story.

What was *instinctive* for the Hebrew family in its past experience had to become more *intentional* for the family in its new reality.

Moses recognized the danger of a compartmentalized faith. He knew that over time the daily relationship with God would be marginalized to a part of the day, then the week, then the month. He suspected there would be a tendency to segment God into an isolated category of life instead of viewing Him as the integrating force that influences *all* of life. He was concerned that society might one day view God as only a smaller part of culture and life.

What Moses says about family seems so commonsense that, at a first glance, you wonder why he even said it. It was actually a remarkably futuristic statement; you would almost think he had a divine revelation about what was coming. (Okay, well, actually, he did.)

His statement transcends every generation. It taps into the potential of families across a variety of cultures. In some ways, what he said about the role of the family may have more meaning to us today than it did to the Hebrew people then. I'm sure some of the parents in that crowd thought, "Isn't that what we have been doing? We have already been talking about this in the morning, through the day, and at night. How can you go through what we went through and not talk about it?"

But things were about to change. They were moving into the Promised Land. If we're honest about our situations, most of us in the West would have to admit that we're pretty much living in a promised land of our own. Few of us have to wander outside our tents each morning and see if the manna has come once again. We have more than almost any other generation in history.

It's characteristic of humans (especially prosperous humans) to create an image of God so narrowly defined that it separates Him completely from culture. Instead of seeing everything as somehow connected to God's story, we love to categorize and segment our faith. Leaders draw man-made lines to separate what is spiritual from what is secular. They create terms and labels to quantify and qualify how God works and how He doesn't. It's almost as if they share the same anxiety Moses had about Canaan.

God will somehow be forgotten.

Eternal truths will be diluted.

The faith of a generation will die.

In some ways, isn't that what's at stake? Isn't that what's happening?

Moses makes a passionate plea to impress on the hearts of children core truths that relate to God's character. Some translations use the phrase "teach diligently." The Hebrew concept of *teach* means "to cause to learn."[1] This is different from a lecture or classroom-based education where a teacher's responsibility ends once the material has been presented. Moses is introducing a systematic teaching process that persists until the core truth is understood and personally embraced.

In other words, he's hoping for actual learning. There is a sobering revelation here about who is ultimately responsible for the stewardship of what is eternally true: It's not Moses or the child but the parents who are ultimately responsible for what should be learned. Family has always been an integral part of God's design.

What Moses set in motion for the Hebrew people was very strategic. *He tapped into the design of creation and leveraged it to nurture a lasting faith.* It's so obvious, it's genius. This principle of rhythm is transferable to every culture throughout all time.

Generally speaking, all people groups get up with the sun, move around in the day, share a meal, and sleep through the night. It's just the way things naturally flow. It's the transcendent pattern of life, this rhythm that establishes a consistent process to challenge the mind and inspire the heart. If the *shema* provides a focus for your relationship (see chapter 4), these instructions for daily life provide the *structure* that enables your relationships to flourish. Moses clearly highlighted certain patterns or times throughout a day that were opportune for teaching.

Look closer at what Moses said in Deuteronomy 6:

> *Impress them on your children. Talk about them when you sit at home and when you walk along the road, when you lie down and when you get up. Tie them as symbols on your hands and bind them on your foreheads. Write them on the doorframes of your houses and on your gates.*[2]

This rhythm cooperates with the way life naturally happens. It's as though a transcendent and perfect God is saying, *I'm not there to simply be put up on a shelf or away in a cabinet and dusted off for special occasions. I want to be part of your everyday life. I'm here for a personal relationship.*

Although every family should look for the patterns that work best for them in light of their schedules, the Orange Factor suggests four specific times from this passage that any family can leverage to build the faith of children and teenagers. Each time seems to lend itself to a different style or approach to learning, and each unique time also presents a different opportunity for the role of a parent.

Consider the following ideas:

Eating meals together is an optimal time to have a focused discussion. It gives parents a specific time to assume the role of a facilitator or teacher to target a specific truth in an interactive and relational context. Mealtime can be effective as an environment to intentionally discuss certain core principles and values as a family in a proactive way. The key word here is *discuss*. So dads, don't get a flip chart out and start listing bullet points for your kids. We have actually organized what we consider to be a variety of activities, discussion starters, and games that can happen once a week before, during, or after mealtime. The goal is for it to be natural and fun, not a teaching platform. We use an interactive system that helps us as a family rotate a dozen or more critical truths creatively that relate to our faith, character, and relationships with others.

Walking or traveling together seems to provide a unique opportunity as well. It is a convenient time to stimulate the kind of informal dialogue that allows kids to drive their own agendas. These times give parents an opportunity to build a relationship through nonthreatening experiences. At some level the parent can actually function as a friend or companion and interpret life together with their children. (Today's cultural mirror to this can be drive time. It has a few enemies, like video games, cell phones, and music, even though creative parents may actually use some of these enemies to generate interesting questions or dialogue.)

Tucking children into bed can also be a meaningful time for families. Too many parents miss the potential of this time because they have a habit of sending their kids to bed rather than taking them. There is something about the private domain of a child's room that gives the parent a chance to have an intimate conversation and become the kind of counselor who listens to the heart of a child. (Have you ever had a child get mad and go to her room and shut the door? It's like she is saying, "I am upset with you and closing you out." The door to your child's room is an important metaphorical door to keep open.)

Getting up in the morning provides a blank page for the family to start fresh relationally. The beginning of a new day has the potential to plant an important emotional seed in the heart of a child. Just a few encouraging words carefully spoken or written can give your children a sense of value and instill purpose. Imagine yourself as a coach, sending your kids into an important game. As a parent you should ask yourself the question, "What can I say or do that will give them fuel to deal with whatever they have to face today?" (Most teachers will tell you they can sense if things went well at home from a child's demeanor when he arrives at school.)

FAMILY TIMES

TIMES	COMMUNICATION	ROLE	GOAL
MEAL TIME	FORMAL DISCUSSION	TEACHER	ESTABLISH VALUES
DRIVE TIME	INFORMAL DIALOGUE	FRIEND	INTERPRET LIFE
BED TIME	INTIMATE CONVERSATION	COUNSELOR	BUILD INTIMACY
MORNING TIME	ENCOURAGING WORDS	COACH	INSTILL PURPOSE

If families decided to take advantage of the times already built into their routines, initiating interaction would be more natural.

Spiritual discussions would be normalized. Doing so moves these important conversations from the formal to the everyday, engaging a rhythm that already exists but leveraging it for the most important purposes.

The return could be enormous. The ancient Hebrew people not only recognized there was a rhythm to their day, but they recognized the rhythms of their week and year as well. They set aside Sabbath once a week for honoring and worshipping God. They set feast days like Passover on the calendar to reflect and celebrate God's faithfulness. This rhythm developed a culture rich with the kinds of traditions that gave context to their story and identity as a people. Most of all, it gave families an opportunity to establish their faith and relationships as a priority. Suddenly, God became a part of everyday life.

To create a rhythm you need to create a priority. A priority is simply a pre-decision about your time. Parents have an advantage when it comes to the issue of time. At least until your children are old enough to drive, you have a window of opportunity to maximize a relationship with your children by the way you handle time.

Think about this: The best churches in your community will average about forty hours in a typical year with your child if he or she is actively involved in most of its programming. Those are important hours where other leaders in the wider circle can influence your child's faith. But there are only forty hours. The average fourth-grade student who goes to church and gets forty hours of influence will spend about four hundred hours that same year playing video games.

What about the time you have at home? While the average church may only have forty hours to influence your child, you as a parent have nearly three thousand hours each year. Don't miss the potential of this detail. We will write it twice to make sure that you don't miss it. You have about three thousand hours that you can use to interact, talk, play, and prioritize with your kids every year. This is why we constantly say to the parents in our churches, "What happens in your house is more important than what happens in church." Simply because of time, you have the potential to influence your children in an incredible way. That is why it is so important for you as a parent to decide in advance what you are going to do with your time.

What happens in your house is more important than what happens in church.

But time alone does not automatically give you the kind of rhythm that will positively influence your children. That influence involves more than just spending time together as a family. Rhythm requires two primary components—intentionality and constancy— and can be defined as a strong, repeated pattern. To create a musical rhythm, an intentional sound must be constantly repeated within a frame of time. If there is no intentional sound, there is no rhythm. If it is not constant, there is no rhythm.

The point Moses is making in this passage parallels the idea of rhythm in the sense that he emphasizes two important things: First, there has to be an effort to make an impression or to communicate what is core and important. Second, the effort should happen repeatedly and establish a pattern over time. The time you spend together as a family should be both interactive and intentional. When both are true, you increase the capacity and influence your time with your children can have.

Quantity of Quality Times

It's not quantity or quality time you need as a family—it's the quantity of quality times. Some would make the case that it is important for families to spend an enormous amount of time together, no matter what they are doing. Others would argue that the issue is not how much time you spend together but how you spend that time. What Moses is suggesting in this passage is that it takes both quantity and quality times working together. When you increase the quantity of quality time you spend together as a family, you leverage your ability to positively impact your children's faith.

> **It's not quantity or quality time you need as a family— it's the quantity of quality times.**

It reminds me (Reggie) of my relationship with our community YMCA. I have a membership. Our offices are next door. I can see it from my window. I am near it every day. It's hard to explain, but sometimes I feel like I stand a better chance of getting in shape because I pay monthly dues and spend a lot of time in close proximity to people who are working out. They have a great lobby and sitting area where I have actually spent time hanging out and working on my laptop. The problem is, spending time near the YMCA doesn't make me healthier. That's the myth of quantity time.

Several years ago, I was feeling guilty because months had passed and I had not done any kind of exercise. So I got up early one morning and went to the YMCA to work out. I wanted to make up for lost time. It felt so positive to finally be doing something productive and to be working out that I became ener-gized. So when I finished doing reps on all the machines, I started over again.

I spent several really good hours putting a lot of effort into the routines and left feeling better about myself. The next morning I woke up in excruciating pain. My damaged muscles had locked up, and I couldn't move. It took a few weeks of therapy before I was normal again. That's the myth of quality time.

Now, YMCAs have a program called Fit Link. When you enter, you log in at a main computer terminal before you start your work-out. That computer is linked to a monitor at every station that records the weight and the number of reps that you lift. It beeps at you if you go too fast or too slow. On your next visit, it calculates what your progress should be based on your last workout and automatically assigns a heavier weight and updated routine to every station. If you skip your workout, it sends a cue to a personal trainer who will email or call you to get you back in your routine. Why? Because someone at the YMCA believes that the only way you can get in shape is to have a good workout on a consistent basis. That's what quantity of quality time means.

It's not enough to spend time together as a family if a family's time together is never meaningful or strategic. It's not just about quantity, and families can't make up for frequently missed opportu-nities by going on a long vacation once a year or by spending several days together during the holidays. And it's not just about quality—families have to be both intentional about how they spend time together and consistent about how often they spend time together. In short, they need to create a rhythm.

Creating Your Rhythm

What's most exciting to us is that God has already established a rhythm that's part of your family life. Everyone eats, travels, goes to bed, and gets up. But in most homes, using those moments for a greater good isn't happening. Integrating spiritual and moral conversation into the equation requires a change for most of us. Because most of us were not raised with the kind of rhythm Moses imagined, it will take some intentionality to leverage those moments for good.

Here are a few practical thoughts we hope will help.

Decide what you want your children to become.

One of the most important questions you can ask as a parent is this: "What do I want my children to ultimately become?" Once you have answered that question, you can back up and look at the discussions and activities in your home in light of that answer.

Jesus was always clarifying the end, keeping those who followed Him focused on what was most important.

Jesus was always clarifying the end, keeping those who followed Him focused on what was most important. He had a way of zeroing in on what really mattered. I wish I could have been there when the Pharisees showed up and started asking questions. The Pharisees loved to flex their spiritual muscles and theological intellect. Anytime they got an opportunity to discredit someone who threatened their identity, they would take their shots. This happens specifically in Matthew 22. After Jesus had silenced the Sadducees, the Pharisees got together to try to trip Him up—"One of them, an expert in the law, tested him with this question: 'Teacher, which is the greatest commandment in the Law?'"[3]

Just think about the situation from God's point of view. Here is Jesus, God in the flesh, being asked a trick question by a Pharisee who was known to be an expert about God. Maybe he had no idea he was talking *to* God. Jesus pulls out a commandment, something He had actually said to Moses on the mountain fifteen hundred years earlier. It had been given a new meaning in Deuteronomy, and now Jesus is about to elevate this passage to an even more significant level: "Love the Lord your God with all your heart and with all your soul and with all your mind. This is the first and greatest commandment."[4]

Did you see what happened? Jesus just pulled a Moses on the Pharisees. Now they are in a tough spot. Not only did He bring up the *shema,* He just promoted it to another level. I'm not sure what happened next, but here's how I imagine it. Maybe a few people clapped. The disciples breathed a sigh of relief. The Pharisees were visibly uncomfortable. There was a dramatic pause.

And then Jesus said, "And …"

Thomas panicked. He was already nervous. He probably thought, *What? There is no "and" after the* shema. *I really wish Jesus would stop messing with what Moses said. Somebody is going to get really mad.* But Jesus continues. He wants to make a point, especially to the Pharisees. So Jesus says, "The second is like it: 'Love your neighbor as yourself.' All the Law and the Prophets hang on these two commandments."[5] Jesus basically adds an addendum to the sacred shema. He establishes three important relationships as priorities: God, others, and self. He tells everyone that their relationships with God affect everything else.

We think there are three issues that relate to this passage that can help parents prioritize what we discuss in our homes and churches. We use the following words to help keep us focused on what we want our kids to become:

- Wonder
- Passion
- Discovery

Love the Lord your God ...

What would happen if your children grew up amazed with the *wonder* of their heavenly Father and how much He loves them? What if they understood God is big enough to handle whatever they will face in life? **You want your children to become people who pursue a relationship with God.**

Love your neighbor ...

What would happen if your kids developed a sense of *passion* that mobilized them to do what Jesus did on earth? What if they understood that they are designed to personally participate in God's story to show His redemptive plan to every generation? **You want your children to become people who love others the way God does.**

...as yourself

What would happen if your children were provoked to pursue a lifestyle of *discovery,* where their identity is determined by a personal relationship with Christ, and where they are guided by His truths? **You want your children to become people who see themselves the way God sees them.**

Jesus claimed that every principle in life comes back to these three relational issues. He amplified what Moses taught and gave us a clear goal for what we want our children to become. This one passage can actually provide a framework for us to use as we create a rhythm to influence our children's faith and character.

Keep thinking Orange.

We've been deep red in this chapter, exploring the heart of home, parenting, and family. You might think we forgot about the church entirely. Not really. Even though the rhythm we're talking about is crafted and lived out at home, the church plays a critical role.

The right church can help you create a rhythm that leads to great moments with your kids.

Remember, when your child is influenced from both directions—the heart of the home plus the light of the church—that's the Orange Factor. Not simply because we are pastors, but also because we are dads, we think it is a great idea for a faith community to be a part of your weekly rhythm. Even one of the Ten Commandments emphasizes the priority of setting aside a day each week to focus on the spiritual side of your family.

The right church can help you create a rhythm that leads to great moments with your kids. The church can be a strategic partner to help you answer questions like, How do you start a spiritual conversation? How do you develop character? What phrases can we use to explain a difficult concept? Churches invest time and resources into teaching kids every week. It's a logical place to tap into for quality resources to teach kids about faith and character.

Synchronize with what your church is teaching.

What if you simply made it a point to learn what your church is teaching and teach that again? What if the three relational issues that Jesus emphasized in Matthew 22 were the focus of your home and church at the same time? A growing number of churches want to help you leverage your influence and create a meaningful rhythm in your home. There is a companion book to *Parenting Beyond Your Capacity* called *Think Orange,* designed to help church leaders develop a ministry style that can sync up with home.

Many churches are no longer sending kids home with smiley-faced paper plates you hang on your refrigerator for a week (and then pitch when they're not looking). As sentimental as they are, the paper plates are giving way to resources designed to help catalyze conversations at home.

Many churches will hand out conversation starters, cards, Bible stories, and even family projects that can help parents and children find something meaningful and strategic to talk about or do together. Often those materials are linked to what your son or daughter is talking about in a small group at church, which allows you as parents to build on what they've already been learning. So use those resources, amplify them, and put them in places to start conversations.

For almost a decade, our reThink organization has provided churches and parents tools to help maximize strategic times in the home to teach kids character and faith. The key issue is how the things we teach on Sunday can be reinforced through the week in the home. For parents to become active in this idea, they really have to embrace the concept that what happens at home is more important than what happens at church.

Be flexible with your rhythm.

The younger your kids are, the more routine life is. It may *feel* out of control, but you will never have more structure than you do with preschoolers. There's also considerable opportunity for a meaningful routine for elementary-school children. Better yet, you tend to have their attention as much as you ever will between kindergarten and the beginning of middle school.

If you have a preschooler or elementary-aged child, applying what we've talked about so far to the rhythm of your family life will be relatively easy. As you think through mealtime, bedtime, morning time, and drive time, you can imagine having some great conversations about faith. It's not that much different from taking time for homework, a family board game, or listening to your favorite songs together. Families do a lot together at this stage. Integrating faith and character into the middle of it is quite natural. When kids are young, structure makes it easy to plan conversations.

Of course, in middle school things begin to change rapidly. To help understand how different ages process life, two of our reThink staff writers (Jon Williams and Greg Payne) have crafted personal ads to illustrate the challenges represented by various grades. It is a fun way to keep us thinking about how our kids are thinking. (You can find more of these on OrangeParents.com.)

Female. 14. DSS (Desperately Seeking Something)
Looking for someone who likes me for who I am as long as they don't mind me not liking them.
Likes: shopping, talking on the phone, movies (if my friends are there), pizza, Bobby Williams

Dislikes: shopping, talking on the phone, movies (if my friends are there), pizza, Bobby Williams

Dream Job: Rescuing kittens or backup dancer to Beyoncé

Personal Goals: To find out who said that I said that I don't like Bobby ... even though I don't ... unless he calls.

Female Parent. 42. DSP (Desperately Seeking Pharmaceuticals)

Looking for text message interpreter, child psychologist, and someone to hold me and tell me, "It's going to be okay."

Likes: Obedience, conversations lasting more than three words, LOVE, KINDNESS, UNDERSTANDING ... I could go on and on.

Dislikes: My child.

Dream Job: Time traveler

Personal Goals: To find the alien race that has abducted my daughter.

As these personal ads illustrate, middle schoolers and teenagers are far more independent and unpredictable. The rhythms that were so easy a few years ago just aren't anymore. As a parent, you have to get more creative. You're just not going to tuck in your fifteen-year-old, and the grogginess of many teenage mornings means breakfast isn't what it used to be.

As a parent, we have to learn to cooperate with our children's natural patterns. There was a huge adjustment for me (Carey) when my eldest son moved into his preteen years. I distinctly remember one day realizing that I wasn't going to be able to play LEGOs with him or his brother forever. I suppose I should have seen that coming, but I really hadn't parented teenagers before. It caught me off guard.

What do you do with teenagers? That's the season that kids pull away from their parents. How do you keep the relationship alive? How do you grow it? Some parents do this instinctively. I didn't.

So I searched for ways to find things they liked doing. We live near a ski hill, so we skied together for a few years. We also live near a lake, so we spent some time on the water together. But you don't ski every day in the winter or head out on the boat every day in the summer. Those activities alone just aren't enough. And day to day, your kids' friends become a bigger and bigger priority to them. You just don't have the same kind of rhythm in the teen years that you do earlier in life.

So you learn a new rhythm. Several aspects of the family rhythms are working particularly well for us at this stage: mealtimes, drive time, and what I call unstructured time. As a family, we have always prioritized dinner. We may not end up with four of us around the table seven nights a week, but we're there most nights, and it's a great time to connect (plus, Toni can really cook, and I have taken up some serious barbecuing). Mealtimes have been a great time to talk about more important things.

But I'm finding that the best and most meaningful conversations with my kids as they've gotten older happen in the car and in unscripted moments. On long drives or trips when there's time to pass, I'll often ask questions or start to turn the conversation toward faith, character, life, and growing up. It probably helps that in a car we're not even making eye contact for the most part. (That helps ease the intensity when you are talking about heavier things.) We've had some wonderful conversations that way.

I've found another great way to be there for my kids is to simply hang around. This is hard for me, because I like to be efficient and productive. But I've found I have to simply unplug and plan to do nothing. Here's what I've discovered: The more I'm around, the more I position myself to allow for moments where meaningful dialogue can happen. There's no direct cause and effect: Being around for four hours doesn't mean anything relationally significant will happen. But the opposite is true: If you're never around, nothing relationally significant will happen. You'll simply miss out.

Strive to create a rhythm that is actually fun for kids.

Recently, our reThink producers met with parents of elementary-aged kids in focus groups and discussed what generates excitement and conversation in the family. What we learned is that when kids get excited about getting something, it generates a better level of interaction. The focus groups resulted in the release of a new concept that is kind of a "cue" box—it cues parents and kids so they will know what to do and when to do it. The interactive box contains a DVD drama and music, collectible resources, and a code that invites kids to continue interacting online with the cast. When any of this content is fun for kids and is synchronized between the church and home, the impact in the heart of the child is greater. Once again, it is the Orange Factor at work.

Regardless of the age of your child, you can be proactive in finding out what they are being taught on Sunday and figuring out how to integrate it into activities or conversations in the rhythm of your family life.

Participate in experiences designed for the family.

Several years ago, I (Reggie) worked with a talented creative team of writers, actors, and musicians to create a weekly experience for families in the Atlanta area that became known as KidStuf. The power of this regular (weekly or monthly) event is that it celebrates family and connects parents in a shared experience. The short program includes an interactive, energetic time of worship and a high-quality storytelling time that appeals to both kids and parents. The music is the kind of music that kids love and parents don't mind listening to. Consistent characters appear in each family experience, making it easy for kids and their parents to connect to characters who become like familiar friends. We called it our Disney approach. The programming is designed so that diverse age groups are engaged and can interact.

Through the years we have learned the benefit of parents and kids having this type of experience. We encourage families to consistently take advantage of any opportunities that are designed for the entire family. These experiences can become effective catalysts for discussion and interaction in the home. Participating with other families in an event is also a great way to celebrate the value of family with kids.

When events are sponsored by a church, they can also become very strategic to synergize the influence of parents and church leaders. Family experiences in churches are different from separated age-graded environments because they're designed for the family to experience them together with other families. It's another way of combining influences to create something greater than either church or family can do on its own, and it expands parents' capacity far beyond what they can do by themselves.

Youth or student family experiences may look different; they can be designed for parents to network and learn. As your children move into the teen years, many student ministry leaders take a more informal approach to partnering with parents. They might host occasional parent nights where leaders talk with parents about various issues. Some leaders provide Web sites or blogs with tips for parents on what student leaders are talking about with your kids or tips about how to chat with your teens. The approach tends to become less structured and more free-flowing during the teen years, but the idea is the same: to help you leverage the time you have with your son or daughter.

Find a rhythm that works for your family.

Keep this in the back of your mind: Don't keep doing something that doesn't work for your family, and don't try to do too much. I hesitate to even make that statement, because most families need to start doing something. It's just that creating a rhythm that works for your family can definitely be tricky. Remember that parents who engage in *small* ways can make a *big* difference in the lives of their kids or teenagers.

Parents who engage in *small* ways can make a *big* difference in the lives of their kids or teenagers.

For example, a mom or dad who spends a few minutes a week in meaningful dialogue reinforcing a principle can help create synergy in a child's learning experiences. It is the power of multiple voices in the life of a child. Parents have to believe in the potential they all have to engage their sons and daughters by creating a rhythm.

The goal is not to do everything,
but to engage in doing something more.

If one dad who hasn't been praying with his
ten-year-old daughter
starts praying with her ...

If one mom who hasn't connected with her
teenage son
convinces him she really cares ...

If one family that rarely discusses spiritual issues starts
talking about God at dinner, even occasionally ...

If anything changes in the rhythm of the home to
remind everyone that God is telling a story through
their family ...

If something that is taught at church is creatively
reinforced at home ...

**... it is more impacting than any parent can
imagine.**

Create a rhythm.

Create a Rhythm

DISCUSSION QUESTIONS

Continue the Conversation

Key Question: *How has spiritual development been part of our family rhythm this week?*

1. When you were growing up, what were some of your favorite family traditions or routines? What were some of the routines or traditions you didn't enjoy? Why were some enjoyable and some not?

2. What rhythms and patterns have you developed within your own family today? How did they originate? What makes them fun? What makes them worthwhile?

3. During your formative years, in what way (if any) was discussion about faith and life integrated into the rhythm of your family life? Would you describe that conversation (or lack of conversation) as healthy? What can you learn from that? How has that impacted the way you approach faith in your own family?

4. Although we have already spent significant time in Deuteronomy 6 in this book, look at it again, reading verses 6–8 closely. Why

do you think Moses picked times like morning time, mealtime, travel time, and bedtime?

5. What kinds of exchanges tend to happen between you and your children during the predictable moments of your day? What can you do to be more intentional at these times with your kids?

6. Think back over your own faith journey and recall some of the most natural and authentic faith conversations you've had with people. What made them powerful for you? What was the setting? How did the conversation get started?

7. What can you learn from the experiences that led to your own spiritual growth that might help you more effectively integrate faith into your family life?

REFLECT: If you are part of a faith community, discuss the kinds of resources your church makes available to you and how you could better leverage them for the purpose of a more intentional rhythm at home.

> *And you must commit yourselves wholeheartedly to these commands that I am giving you today. Repeat them again and again to your children. Talk about them when you are at home and when you are on the road, when you are going to bed and when you are getting up. (Deut. 6:6–7 NLT)*

CHAPTER SEVEN

Family Value #5: Make It Personal

Put yourself first when it comes to personal growth.

So … do you remember who Moses was talking to in Deuteronomy 6? The reason we ask this question is because we intentionally skipped something Moses said, so we could bring it up right now. We took it out of the order it appeared in the actual text to highlight it here at the end of the book so it will be one of the first things you think about as you finish. This family value is a little different than the first four you've read. This one is about *your relationship with you.*

Moses said something so quickly in Deuteronomy 6 that it is easy to miss it. Right after he talked about loving God and right before he talked about leveraging your time, he said something that pivots everything else. It is very relevant to your ability to influence beyond your capacity. He said, "These commandments that I give you today are to be upon your hearts."[1]

Did you notice it? It was just two words: *your hearts*. What was Moses implying? Moses was explaining that this has to be in you as a parent before you can expect it to be in your children. The most important thing that happens as a result of reading this book may not be what happens in the lives of your children, but what happens in your life.

The most important thing that happens as a result of reading this book may not be what happens in the lives of your children, but what happens in your life.

For me (Reggie), the race to nowhere started at age seventeen. I took extra courses in high school, played varsity baseball, worked two jobs, and traveled with a music group. When my grades started slipping, my Latin teacher confronted me after class. Mrs. Culbreth said, "If you don't slow down, you're gonna burn out by thirty." I laughed, patted her on the shoulder, and got busy doing more important stuff.

I remember wondering as I walked away, "Why thirty?"

I completely forgot about what she said until I was thirty-one, sitting in a car late one night on an Alabama dirt road. I had come to a dead end emotionally. Mrs. Culbreth had missed it by only one year.

That night her words drifted back into my mind from more than a decade earlier. How did she know? What was it she saw in me? She had definitely been a prophet, and my life was imploding. I will spare you the details of the ministry I was attempting to manage and the countless hours I had spent working, creating, and investing in teenagers and young adults. To make matters more challenging, my wife and I were at a stage of family life when we were parenting four children under the age of seven.

On that back road, all of that faded away, and I was overwhelmed with loneliness and emptiness. The collapse happened subtly. I found out in counseling over the next few months what Mrs. Culbreth had tried to tell me. We all enter into adulthood with a certain amount of reserve. If we expend too much without making deposits, we find ourselves at an emotional deficit.

My childhood was great. I lived in a neighborhood where every house was lit up for Christmas. We climbed trees and played baseball in front yards. Frequent trips to visit relatives would mean spending all day hiking through the woods, fishing, and exploring old barns. I spent numerous weekends at nearby lakes, rode dirt bikes, and enjoyed quality time with our church youth group. It was Camelot for me. Every walk, every friend, every Sunday, every trip, and every game made a deposit in my invisible personal bucket.

So I started the journey out of high school feeling like I had a bank full of energy. Then my life moved into warp speed, and I began to burn fuel at a pretty high rate. Mrs. Culbreth was just estimating how long it would take me to burn a full tank at the rate I was moving.

The problem was that I did not realize the hidden value that seventeen years of positive deposits had made into my personal emotional account. I just started spending emotionally without making deposits. Then one day when I was facing a personal crisis, I reached into my emotional bank, and it was empty.

In the difficult months that followed, I wasn't the only one who suffered. It was like the traffic backed up on a bridge behind a car that's out of gas. A line of people I cared about were also affected. Thankfully, I was surrounded by a few friends and family members who cared enough to rescue me. They were committed to making new deposits in my life and helping me restore what I had lost.

It is not difficult to understand what happened.

I had simply failed to refuel my private world.

I was leading others, just not myself.

I had totally depleted my capacity because I neglected to nurture my personal growth.

A crucial link exists between your ability to parent and your personal growth.

The fifth parenting value—making it personal—is going to challenge you as a parent in a way the other values don't. You could embrace the other four values we discuss in this book (widen the circle, imagine the end, fight for the heart, and create a rhythm) in just the way described but still miss something critical here.

This one's *personal*. It's not actually so much about your kids. This one will *benefit* your kids, for sure. But it's not directly about them. This one's about *you*.

That's why it's so important for you to hang out in this chapter for a while. In a very real way, making it personal will help every other step you take as a parent.

Now because this is about you, and because your life is incredibly busy, this parenting value could be the one you are most tempted to *skip*. After all, that's what parents do. We set aside our wants and needs so our kids can get ahead.

But this time, that would be a serious mistake.

To understand how essential this is, we need to look at how we parent and why we need to take a break from that to make this journey more personal.

When it comes to character and faith, your kids are *watching* you in a way they might not watch you in other pursuits. Because it's so personal, you can't *do* faith and character *for* your kids. There's another factor at work.

If you want it to be in them, it needs to be in you.

If it's not in you, they know it. When it comes to spiritual and character formation, your journey impacts them deeply. If you want it to be in them, it needs to be in you.

Kids Can Sense It

If you are merely trying to instill faith and morals for the sake of the kids, but it's not a priority personally, they'll eventually catch on. Kids have an amazing fake detector. I (Carey) learned this when my kids were very young and we were trying to get them to eat vegetables.

I have an aversion to broccoli. I'd like to call it an allergy, but that would be lying. It's not an allergy. It's just an extreme dislike of the stuff. I don't actually admire anything in the broccoli family. Cabbage, brussels sprouts, cauliflower … that entire food family makes me wonder why these vegetables were created. I know there are people who sincerely love those foods, but they must have been paid large sums of money by grocery stores to try to move produce.

So we had some interesting times in our home when we were trying to get our toddlers to eat nutritiously. My wife, Toni, wanted me to model a good diet, so I took one for the team.

One night as the food was being passed around the table, Toni and I extolled the virtues of vegetables, how good they are for you, how important they are to your diet. That night, everyone was going to have some, including me.

I put the broccoli on my fork. I held my breath. I tried to smile. I gulped. The questions started immediately—"How come Dad only has a little bit? How come his face went all crooked when he ate it? If Dad doesn't like to eat it, why do we have to?"

Small children are actually quite intelligent.

You've already seen that at work in your family. Your kids know when it's real. They know when it's not. If you're really good, you might be able to convince them faith and character are important. But eventually they'll begin to sense whether or not those things actually important *to you*.

Just like children can spot a small difference of opinion between parents and crack it open wide enough to sometimes get their way, they can also tell quite readily when you say one thing but live another.

If faith isn't personal, it becomes as easy to hang up as a pair of cleats when the extra practices have lost their luster. Worse, kids can see faith as something they outgrow around the time Webkinz or LEGOs give way to weekends away with friends.

That's why your personal growth is so important. When it comes to spiritual and moral development, your children are watching you with laserlike focus.

As you read this, your anxiety level is probably rising. You feel like you can't possibly measure up. If you were to level with your kids about your fears, your inconsistencies, or even how shaky your faith is on some days, you'd feel like you were admitting defeat.

But that's a perfect-picture mind-set again, isn't it? God is interested in writing a bigger story, and your personal growth is part of the plotline. In fact, your developing story may be more influential than you think.

That's why parents need to let their kids see them struggle to grow. They need to see your authenticity and hear your transparency. Most of all, they need to observe up close that your spiritual, moral, and relational **Whatever you want your children to become, you should honestly strive to become as well.** growth is a priority in your life. This is not about a perfect model, just an honest one. Whatever you want your children to become, you should honestly strive to become as well.

- If you want them to make church a priority, then you should go.
- If you want them to respect leaders, then watch your attitude.
- If you want them to admit their mistakes, then say you're sorry.
- If you want them to work hard, then be an involved volunteer.
- If you want them to be generous, then give freely yourself.
- If you want them to pursue God, then get alone with God.
- If you want them to be honest, then treat others with integrity.

Most of all, whenever you make a mistake (and you will), just admit it and start over.

It Has to Be in You

That's why Moses pointed out how important it was for faith to start with parents. A legacy is contagious. Moses says you are to "love the Lord your God with all your heart" and that God's principles should be "in your hearts." Moses is setting up the adult population of Israel to understand how to pass faith on to the next generation. We know this because he goes on to tell them to "impress" these commands on their children.

Let's look closer at Deuteronomy 6 so we remember the context:

First, Moses establishes God as the cornerstone of the Israelites' identity.

Then, Moses challenges them to pursue a love relationship with God as the basis for how they live.

Next, to make sure they don't miss the contagious nature of their legacy, he reminds the Israelites that these things have to be in *their* hearts before they can hand them off to their children. If you are a parent, this is the basic principle—**it has to be in *you* before it can be in *them*.**

Moses implies that before you can ask who your children are becoming, you have to examine who *you* are becoming. It would fundamentally change the way we look at our lives if we really believed the greatest thing that could happen in the heart of a child would be what happened in the heart of a parent.

Again, it is counterintuitive: *If the target is to pass a personal faith along to children, parents should make it a priority to make faith personal in their own lives.*

So how do you do that when you are not sure about what's in you? How do you handle it when what's in you is less than you desire for yourself and less than you desire for your kids?

I (Reggie) know some things are in me that I don't want my kids to catch. What am I supposed to do about those things? I have this dilemma. On one hand, I don't think I am ready for my children to pick up even my most positive virtues. I'm just not finished learning yet. My faith is not quite strong enough, and my character isn't as spotless as it should be. On the other hand, I am nervous because there is this list of other quirky issues I have that I don't want to hand down. So in both ways, I struggle.

Truthfully, I have never met a parent who claimed to be ready to parent when the first child was born. The National Center for Health Statistics reports the average age of first-time moms is twenty-five.[2] That's how old I was when we had our first child. I am speaking for myself and not my wife when I say I learned by trial and error, and there were a lot of errors. Admit it, if you're middle-aged, you cringe when you think about what you were like in your twenties. We grow as parents by practicing parenting. We are not experts before we start—we test our theories out on our kids.

This is different from anything else you do. You can find a dancing instructor before you do it in public, a coach for baseball before you play an official game, and a degree or training before you start a career. But no university offers a major in parenting. You don't get to go to a room somewhere and practice parenting before you have to really do it. In his book *Outliers*, Malcolm Gladwell points out that someone needs ten thousand hours of practice to become truly good at a particular task.[3] We start as parents with exactly zero hours.

There is not even a dress rehearsal. You're just supposed to know how to be a parent. The assumption is that your parents parented you, so now you have a model to parent your kids, and your kids will parent their kids based on how you parented them.

Everything doesn't have to be right in you or about you before you can be a positive influence in your children's lives.

Faith and character both develop over time. We are in process. We aren't there yet. And yet who we are already impacts our kids one way or the other. How we pursue God, how we love our spouses, how we treat others, how we respond to authority, how we spend our money, how we work, and how we communicate will all affect their values and perspectives. The dilemma most of us face is that we don't have the margin or luxury to get all of those things right before we start parenting.

Our only viable solution is to do what all wise and loving parents do with their weaknesses—cover them up! Bury them so deep that our kids will never find them. And many of us try exactly that.

Sooner or later, those weaknesses surface.

Never try to impress your kids with who you want them to think you are. They will be disappointed that you were never able to admit your struggles and weaknesses. I have never said, "I really struggle with _____" and had my wife and kids say, "Oh really? I didn't know that." They know. They watch you every day, so you might as well admit the weaknesses you are asking God to work on in your life. It's okay for them to see who you really are, especially if you want them to see the difference God is making in your life.

Moses was not suggesting that parents live a perfect example or model. He was not implying that until you obey all of the commandments, you can't expect to pass on your faith. He was saying that these truths need to be "upon your hearts." This is about desire and passion. Everything doesn't have to be right in you or about you before you can be a positive influence in your children's lives. But there is one thing you have to embrace if you hope to have lasting influence: You have to be authentic. You have to make it personal.

A Front-Row Seat

Your kids already have a front-row seat to your life. The question is, what are they watching? Is it just show? Or is it a real-life adventure where they see courage and passion to overcome personal obstacles? What if your personal growth was a front-row seat to the bigger story God wants to write in your family?

> **Your kids already have a front-row seat to your life. The question is, what are they watching?**

Show them what it is like to pursue a fuller relationship with God and your spouse. Show them how it looks to prioritize Jesus above anything else. Show them what it is like to reject the materialism and consumerism of our culture. If you want your children to have it in them, they have to see it in you.

Your kids need to see you ...

> ... struggle with answers.
> ... face your weaknesses.
> ... deal with real problems.
> ... admit when you are wrong.
> ... fight for your marriage.
> ... resolve personal conflict.

Your children need to see you make relational, emotional, and spiritual growth in your life a priority. If you don't make it personal for yourself, it may never be personal for them.

Some of our favorite stories have been told by children of single parents who watched their moms or dads overcome difficult obstacles. These single moms and dads parented beyond their capacity because they allowed God to write a story on their heart, a story of redemption and restoration.

Your kids can't see who you are becoming if they never see who you really are. And if they never see who you are, how will they know the difference God has made and continues to make in your life? It is the firsthand look at that difference that will give them hope for their future and faith in what God can do in them.

I (Carey) taught a series on the tension between men and women. I opened the first week by explaining that over nineteen years of marriage, Toni and I have disagreed over every subject imaginable and even managed to invent a few new ones. Not only is it true, it's strangely helpful. It relaxes people when they hear that the pastor doesn't have it all together. It puts the message in reach of everyone in the room. It makes us feel like we're all in this together (which we are). It even makes people think, *If there's hope for the pastor, there might be hope for me.* I also share successes along the way but not without simultaneously sharing the struggles.

When you're watching your favorite athlete being interviewed, your ears perk up when you get behind-the-scenes information. Even more than the public image, you want to hear about how he grew up, what home was like, what fears he has, what hopes he has, and what he battles with daily. *Off*-the-record conversation is almost always more compelling than *on*-the-record conversation. When you learn to admit your limited capacity and parent out of your weakness, you turn the spotlight on God's capacity. Again and again, the Bible communicates the theme that out of our weaknesses, God is made strong.

Transparency has an appropriate place and time and should be moderated by common sense, but most of us would benefit from sharing more than we do. Being honest gives people, especially our children, a front-row seat to see the grace of God active and alive.

So How Do I Do This?

How do you make it personal? The answer is not complicated. In our organization, we have a number of staff members with young children. Some of you may be in that phase of parenting where your children are preschoolers or early-elementary students. This age is marked by total dependence on the parent, and it can be overwhelming at times. One of the mothers on our staff mentioned in passing, "I wish I could have one day a month for myself." When we asked why she didn't take that day, she responded, "I would feel so guilty." It feels selfish. It feels inconsiderate. The unselfish truth, though, is that making time to put deposits into your emotional, intellectual, relational, or spiritual bank ultimately benefits everyone you love.

Jesus did it. And He was perfect. He was God. But He was also human. And He was smart enough to know that the human side of His nature needed to be nurtured occasionally. Jesus consistently withdrew from the crowds. Sometimes He would just disappear. Often it was to pray, sometimes to hang out with His close friends, and occasionally just to take a nap on the boat. Even Jesus carved out time to refuel. He recognized the value of making personal deposits in His emotional and spiritual bank account.

Is it possible that you're the kind of parent who feels guilty if you take a break? Maybe you run a long time because you have more capacity than most. It is possible to be close to empty and not know it. The question is, what kind of consistent deposits are you making in your personal life, for the sake of your family life?

In *The Price of Privilege*, family psychologist Madeline Levine says, "Our best shot at good parenting comes when we have enough internal resources of our own to make it through tough patches— this means friends, interests, sources of support, clear priorities, and clarity about our own life story."[4]

Is it possible that there is a crisis coming around the corner and you are setting yourself up to go into debt emotionally? Everyone is different, but it is important to understand enough about yourself, your capacity, your tastes, and your personality to identify the kind of deposits that fuel you. You should spend some time evaluating yourself personally, identifying those things that restore your emotions and inspire you to grow.

Spiritual Deposits

The more time we spend reflecting, praying, preparing, and even resting, the better fathers, husbands, mothers, wives, leaders, and friends we become. We can learn more. We trust God more. It shapes our character and our spirit.

Just like there's not a perfect picture for the family, there's not a single picture of what our spiritual growth time looks like either.

Most of us who have been around church see value in praying and reading the Bible. And

Just like there's not a perfect picture for the family, there's not a single picture of what our spiritual growth time looks like either.

there is tremendous value in building an ongoing conversation with your heavenly Father and in getting to know the Scriptures. But there are a variety of ways to get to know God better. One of our concerns in a chapter like this is that some will assume building a relationship with God means following a certain rigid model of spiritual growth. To make true spiritual deposits in our lives, we may need to explore more personalized spiritual paths.

Some of us grow by worship, giving, caring, nature, silence, simplicity, or action. Most of us would respond to a mixture of these models. It's almost like spiritual cross-training. Most important in all of this is that our love for our heavenly Father grows and our relationship with Him deepens. *How* that happens can vary.

I (Carey) know that my wife, Toni, finds closeness to God in nature. She loves time alone in the Bible, but there's something about being among rocks, trees, water, and blue sky that draws her closer to God. It actually draws her in spiritually.

Now I like nature, but it doesn't speak to my soul nearly as much as it does hers. In fact, being in the heart of a big city and watching people, technology, and progress stimulates my theological thinking more than a walk in the woods. This is likely evidence that my wife is far more spiritual than I am, or it might just mean that God created us differently but loves us the same. One size does not fit all when it comes to the ways we connect with God most deeply and personally.[5]

As you begin to prioritize personal time with God, make sure you discover how you grow best. Realize that your relationship with God will become more passionate as you become more passionate about how you connect with Him.

There are days where we do things we don't want to do now so we can do what we want to do later. But eventually, disciplines can become passions. Some of you started running for exercise out of discipline and struggled for a season. Now, you love running so much that if you don't get a run in, you become distressed.

It can be that way with spiritual growth. When you find the paths that best fit your wiring, spiritual growth is not only healthy, it can be deeply rewarding.

Think about what you might have to *stop* doing so you can start prioritizing your personal growth.

Because our lives are

so incredibly full, don't necessarily think in terms of adding time to your schedule. Think about what you might have to *stop* doing so you can start prioritizing your personal growth. You actually will have the time to develop personally if you approach it in this way.

Not all of your personal-growth time has to be spent alone. Some of the time we spend on growth comes in the form of dialoguing with those around us to learn where God might most need to strengthen us. That's where relational deposits come in.

Relational Deposits

In the sense that none of us have the capacity to successfully parent all by ourselves, keeping a focus on your connection with friends and family members is essential. One of the most important deposits you'll make for your well-being begins when you begin investing in relationships with others.

Be strategic about friends.

We are relational creatures. Some of you are wired to enjoy the crowd, while others of you are wired to hang out with one or two people. The point is we need people in our lives. The right friends are a source of fuel for our souls, hearts, and minds.

Gordon McDonald wrote a book in which he grouped people according to their contributions to your personal world. Some people are VIPs or Very Important People. Others are VRPs or Very Resourceful People. There is even a category of VDPs or Very Draining People.[6] It is easy to become surrounded by the people who take away our emotional energy instead of becoming intentional about doing life with a number of people who are committed to inspiring and fueling us. For the sake of your children, it is important to be in relationships with the right kinds of people. If you made a list of those you spend time with right now, who would you say are the inspiring and fueling types? How are you organizing your month or week to spend time with them?

Find a community of parents.

One important way to make relational deposits is by establishing a small group or community of parents that meets frequently. Many churches have created opportunities for adults to connect on a weekly or biweekly basis for the purpose of spiritual and personal growth. Doing life with other adults who represent your season of life can be a very fueling activity.

One important way to make relational deposits is by establishing a small group or community of parents that meets frequently.

Whether your church hosts these groups or they develop organically within your faith community, they can be vital to your personal growth. This is another way you parent beyond your capacity—when you network and learn with other parents. We cannot imagine what our journeys as parents would be like without countless meaningful conversations with other parents who share the common values of this book.

We both have worked to develop an approach to church based on the Orange philosophy, a style of church that partners with parents on multiple levels to help them integrate these principles.

We are convinced that a key to every parent's personal growth is a willingness to network with a consistent small group of adults to gain spiritual and relational insight. People need people, and parents need parents.

When families share these values collectively, it establishes a clear strategy for the parents to partner with the church. At OrangeParents.com, we provide podcasts and resources to help parents who want to continue to learn and discuss these issues. Many of these elements can be used in the context of a small-group environment. We would strongly urge you as a parent to consider building a relationship with a community of parents that will help you continue to grow.

Date your spouse.

If you are married, one of the greatest gifts you can give to your children is a healthy relationship with your spouse. One way to make it personal is to model the right kind of romance and friendship with your partner. The pressure in your home will be for everything to become focused on the needs of the kids. If you are not careful, this could lead to a mind-set that they are the center of the home. Your kids should grow up with a sense that your spouse is your priority relationship.

One of the best ways to build security and confidence in your children is to constantly strengthen your marriage relationship. Don't underestimate the importance of a child seeing a mother and father engaged in a friendship and interacting in an affectionate way.

It is possible to parent beyond your capacity simply by leaving your children for an evening to go spend time together as a couple.

I (Reggie) saw this modeled in one of the first pastors with whom I served, Larry Thompson. He and his wife, Cynthia, were committed to dialoguing daily, dating weekly, and departing on a just-the-two-of-them retreat at least once a year. Their two daughters grew up seeing Cynthia prepare for their Friday-night dates, sometimes even helping her with fashion choices or making restaurant suggestions. The girls knew that Friday night was a priority for their parents.

Your spouse was there before your children, and he or she will be there long after your children have left. It's wise to do your part to keep that relationship thriving.

Starting Now

So how does one begin to incorporate this into the routine of daily life? The only way we know to make personal growth happen is to make it a priority.

Our in-boxes fill up hourly. Most of our days have more tasks than time. Family needs a quantity of quality time if you're really going to build a relationship that's deep and lasting. There are many compelling reasons not to prioritize personal growth.

In the last chapter, we talked about creating a rhythm for your family. But maybe you are at a place where you need to wrestle with this question: What personal-growth rhythm will you create for yourself? The rhythm will look different in different people's lives.

You'll need to decide which personal rhythm works best for you. Our suggestion is to give this kind of development your prime time, whether it's morning or another time.

What's prime time for you? How can you give some of your best time and energy over to your personal development? You'll likely have to rearrange your day. What will you move? What will you stop doing so you can start doing this? If you're currently not doing this, what about starting with five minutes a day? If you are in the habit of making space for personal growth, what could you do to change it or enrich it?

Making It Personal

As you start to make personal growth a priority, something amazing will happen. Your kids will notice. Remember: you are the greatest influence in their lives.

God will start to write a bigger story in your life. You will begin to change, grow, and develop. You will have given your kids a developing story to see firsthand. And they will know it's authentic.

Authentic stories are the hardest ones to argue away. They tend to draw us in because we can identify more easily with where people struggle than we can where we pretend to succeed.

When you make it personal, the story lives in you, and it's much easier for that story to one day be in them.

A few years ago I (Carey) made a change that helped me turn a corner. I simply stopped saying (to myself and others), "I don't have the time for that." Ever find yourself saying that? Stop it. Seriously. Just don't say that anymore.

God gives me the same amount of time in the day as everyone else on

When you make it personal, the story lives in you, and it's much easier for that story to one day be in them.

the planet. Jesus got twenty-four hours in a day. The people I admire most, who accomplish far more than I do, get the same twenty-four hours a day. They just spend their time differently. I learned that if I want a different outcome, I need to learn how to spend time differently.

So I stopped saying, "I don't *have* the time." Instead, I started saying, "I didn't *make* the time." That made me realize that everything I do is a choice. It's a constant reminder to me that I need to *make* time for what's important and cut what isn't.

Take your calendar out right now and look at the next week. There are only a few things you *need* to do. You likely need to sleep, eat three times a day, and perhaps show up for work. Pretty much everything else is a choice. You are authoring your own destiny.

For me, it means the first moments of the morning—usually in the living room with my Bible, some prayer time, and some real stillness in the house. If I miss a morning, I usually notice that my relationship with God and others suffers. For me, it also means making time for personal reflection outside of my devotion time.

Increasingly, this means seeking feedback from others about what I'm doing well and what I'm not doing so well. My wife is my best confidante and most loving critic. She has a window into my soul and can identify issues to which I'm blind. I also solicit feedback from friends and coworkers. Their input helps me become a better person. More recently, my desire to grow personally has even included regular exercise and diet changes. Being in better physical shape seems to have an impact on being in better relational and emotional shape.

Finally (and you can't script or plan this one), I listen to my kids. Because we've tried to foster a more honest dialogue in my home, my kids will call me up on issues from time to time. Both of my sons are teenagers. As you may know, teens will tell you exactly what they think, even when you're not asking. Every time they give me feedback, I have a choice. Will I ignore it because I'm too busy or don't want to hear it (done that), or will I stop, engage it, and grow from it (occasionally done that, too)? It can be a great and humbling moment to discuss with your child where you need to grow as a parent.

Time to Stop

Those who were about to cross into the Promised Land would be tempted by many good ways to fill their time. With all that milk and honey and all those grapes, the inhabitants of Israel might find themselves filling up on what was right in front of them without looking for better options. Moses knew this, and he intentionally spoke in his send-off message about making the right decisions—for ourselves and for our families. Choosing to make personal growth a priority means we start looking for better options. You may have to stop doing a few things so you can start focusing on what's most likely to lead you into a deeper place spiritually.

Doing so will bring some surprising outcomes. It will build your relationship with God. But here's what else might happen: You will discover that by prioritizing what matters most, you end up with *more* time. Well, maybe not more time, but more margin. As you grow, you will be better able to cut the unnecessary clutter out of your life. You will begin to sort through the issues that both positively and negatively affect your capacity. You'll tend to learn what's most important because you're doing more important things, more important for your heart so it can be in the hearts of your children.

Make It Personal

DISCUSSION QUESTIONS

Continue the Conversation

Key Question: *Is my relationship with God growing, authentic, and personal?*

1. Sometimes it's hard to remember life before children. Did you have more time for yourself back then? What were some of your favorite things to do to get reenergized?

2. How do you spend your days? Make a quick list of all the things you typically do in just one day. Which ones require the most energy and time? Is anything on the list something that fills you and energizes you as an individual and not just as a parent?

3. Spend a few moments reflecting on the times in your Christian journey when you felt closest to God. What were you doing, or what was happening at the time that made you feel this way?

4. What can you do to intentionally recreate these times? Write down your plan.

5. Many times it helps to partner with your spouse or another parent to take turns watching the kids so you can get away for a while. Make sure to tell your kids what you're doing or where you're going. It's important for them to see you making your relationship with God a priority.

6. Talk with your children about the times they feel closest to God. Is it when they pray? When you tuck them in at night? When they are playing outside? When they are at church? Write these times on the family calendar so they can see that investing in your relationship with God is a priority in your family.

Read Deuteronomy 6:4–6.

> *Listen, O Israel! The LORD is our God, the LORD alone. And you must love the LORD your God with all your heart, all your soul, and all your strength. And you must commit yourselves wholeheartedly to these commands that I am giving you today. (NLT)*

REFLECT: How would the way you spend your time look different if you took these verses to heart? Why is the health and growth of your personal relationship with God important to your children? If you were to summarize this passage for your kids, what would you say?

Faith Skills

Many churches are teaching targeted faith skills for children. But it's also important for us as parents to be able to navigate these skills, because it has to be in us before it's in them. This can be part of your spiritual growth.

Navigate the Bible (survey and locate)

The Bible is a mystery to a lot of us, but our hope is that you can begin to see it as a gift and even a friend. As you begin to get to know the Bible well, you'll discover that it's far more practical than most people think. A great way to get into the Bible is to find a reading plan that fits your personal rhythm and needs. The people at YouVersion.com make it easy. Online or on your smart phone, you can access many translations of the Bible and more than a dozen reading plans that will take you through all parts of the Bible on a schedule. It's also free. Having a reading plan can help you navigate the Bible for the first time or the hundredth time with meaning and purpose.

Personalize Scripture (memorize and apply)

Knowing the Bible is one thing, but learning to apply it is another. We know a lot of things in life (carrot sticks are better for you than potato chips), but we know far more than we ever apply. The real value of knowledge comes in the application. If your goal is to lose weight, knowing that carrots are healthy is one thing. But it won't help you unless you eat them instead of the potato chips.

Knowing Scripture can (and should be) a journey in discovery. If you find a verse or passage particularly helpful, try memorizing it. But even more than that, begin to apply what you know. Ask God and talk to others about how to make some of the changes you know need to happen in your life. When you apply what you know, you really begin to grow.

Dialogue with God (private and public)

Prayer can seem formal and stiff to a lot of us. To others, it's so casual it only happens on the drive to work or while sorting laundry. The truth is somewhere in between. As a parent, begin to think of prayer like a conversation between friends. As the substance of a relationship, prayer becomes alive.

Just like human relationships grow or die based on how we communicate, so our spiritual journeys are deeply impacted by how we learn to communicate with God. As your personal prayer life grows, it will become easier to pray at mealtimes, bedtimes, and other times with your children.

Articulate Faith (share and defend)

One of the best ways to learn something is to teach it. Try it with math. Most teachers discover this: You end up learning more because you teach. As you talk about your faith with friends, with your kids, with your spouse, and with coworkers, you'll be amazed to discover that your faith grows and gets stretched as a result.

Worship with Your Life (praise and give)

Faith isn't just about an idea. It's about a relationship that expresses itself throughout life. Forgiveness is at the heart of the Christian message, and when we are forgiven, we become grateful. As your gratitude for faith grows, you'll find you want to express it in many ways. You might want to sing, you may want to verbalize your thanks, and you'll want to give more fully of yourself.

These five Faith Skills are a beginning (for you and for your kids), but they'll be completed by the deposits you make relationally and intellectually.

CHAPTER EIGHT

Back to the Story

You can moblize your family to demonstrate God's love in a broken world.

As parents, we are ready to contend for our children's safety as soon as they are born. We buy veritable plastic straitjackets and buckle our kids into car seats, construct beds and play zones with virtual prison bars, hook their arms to an expandable leash to walk through the mall, and install video surveillance systems so our children can be monitored from every room. As parents, we are programmed to protect. We feel responsible to ensure we have the kind of boundaries that will make the world childproof. Between parenting magazines and pediatricians, we become convinced that our primary job is to protect our children, so we make rules, set limits, and put up fences. That's what we are supposed to do as parents, right?

> **It's possible to hold on to our kids so tightly that we forget the ultimate goal of parenting is to let go.**

Our natural instinct is to insulate, isolate, segregate, and separate our kids from everything we think might be a threat.

The truth is, it's possible to hold on to our kids so tightly that we forget the ultimate goal of parenting is to let go. There's a danger in caring more about our children's protection than we do about providing them with a meaningful purpose. There is a danger in caring more about our children's safety than we do their faith. When we become overly preoccupied with our children's immediate physical and even emotional well-being, we can end up robbing them of necessary experiences, life lessons, and opportunities.

When we parent from our protective instincts, we're fine if our children never climb a mountain as long as it guarantees they never get hurt. But what if your children were made for the mountains? They might be safe in the lowlands, but will they be who God made them to be? What if they were supposed to learn to climb those mountains early on, while they still had a safety net at home? What happens to their passion? What happens to their hearts? What if your children were made for something more? If you are a parent remember this:

> The mission of the family is not ultimately to protect your children
> but to mobilize them to demonstrate God's love to a broken world.

What does that have to do with parenting beyond your capacity? Everything! If your primary goal is to keep your children close instead of letting them go, then your capacity will limit your children's potential. You will chain them to your limitations, to your weaknesses, to your experiences, to *your* role in God's story, not theirs. You have to remind yourself frequently that the day your child was born, you began preparing him or her to leave your home.

Mobilizing your child doesn't mean your family won't share a mission together. It doesn't mean you are not all connected to the same story. It just means that your child needs to have room to discover his or her unique and individual role.

As we've discussed parenting from a bigger-story perspective, we've explained how God desires to write something incredible in your family's life. If you parent from the bigger-story perspective, you instill within your children a sense of adventure that engages their hearts. You invite them to experience things that are beyond your individual capacity to help them experience.

A couple of years ago at our Orange Conference, Donald Miller shared a story about a friend who was having problems with his daughter. The dad was worried because the daughter had gotten involved in a gothic lifestyle and was dating a guy who was bad news. As a frustrated dad, his technique for dealing with the situation was to yell at her and make her go to church. When he came to Don for advice, Don told him, "I think what your daughter is doing is choosing a better story."

He went on, "We're all designed to live inside a story. Your daughter was designed to play a role in a story. In the story she has chosen, there is risk, adventure, and pleasure. She is wanted, and she is desired. In your story, she's yelled at, she feels guilty, and she feels unwanted. She's just choosing a story that is better than the one you're providing. Plus, in the midst of placing her in an awful story, you make her go to church. So you're associating a bad, boring story with God, who has a great story. Don't do that anymore. You have to tell a better story."

The dad became inspired, and within a week he made contact with a small village in Mexico that needed an orphanage. The orphanage was going to cost about $25,000, so he proposed to his family that they raise the money. He painted the picture for them: "Here's the deal, you guys. I found this village in Mexico that needs an orphanage. Awful things may happen to these kids if they don't have a place to go, so I think we need to build this orphanage as a family. It's going to cost over $25,000, and I know we don't have any money, but we need to do it within two years."

He brought out a whiteboard and asked his family—who all thought he had lost his mind—for ideas. Then his daughter piped up and said, "I have a MySpace page and lots of friends. Maybe we can use that." Ideas came from everywhere. "We're going to have to go to Mexico, because if we're going to do this, we need to see the village." "I know an architect." "Maybe we can get some supplies donated." "I've got a new camera; I can take pictures of the kids in the orphanage." "And we're all going to need passports."

What's happening here? They were getting caught up in a real story with risk and adventure. Not long after, the girl broke up with her boyfriend. Why? Because she found a better story. Her new story let her play the heroine. She had an opportunity to sacrifice and give of herself to accomplish something that would make a lasting impact. She felt wanted and needed in this story.

> The heart will gravitate toward
> whatever offers adventure and significance.

The bottom line is that children need to experience something bigger than themselves. Whether or not we provide them with the opportunity to do so, they will look for a way to participate in something adventurous.

Generations of kids have abandoned Christianity because it was defined for them in terms that were static and noneventful. That's why it's up to us to think creatively about encouraging our children to engage in consistent personal ministry opportunities during their most formative years.

Think about the experiences that have had the most impact on your faith. Think about the times in your life when you realized that God could use you to accomplish something meaningful.

As we look back on pivotal moments in our lives, some of the greatest chapters unfolded only after we took the biggest risks. We are attracted to a dramatic storyline of faith in other people's lives. Like you, we're attracted to people who overcome exceptional odds. Hollywood makes billions off stories like that. It's also what makes biblical stories so compelling. Think of three Jewish teenagers in a foreign land staring down a furnace so hot it kills the soldiers guarding it. Could God possibly deliver them? No one would have guessed that they'd emerge without a singe.

Or try this: Imagine you and your family with a large body of water in front of you and the military might of a global superpower zoning in on you from behind. The only question would be, *So how are we going to die? Are we going to drown or get slaughtered?*

God appears to specialize in inviting people beyond their personal capacity so He can show His power.

Nobody in that moment is thinking the sea is going to part, even though moments later, it would.

It's in those dramatic storylines that God does His greatest work. God appears to specialize in inviting people beyond their personal capacity so He can show His power. He calls us to trust, to risk, and to believe beyond what we can control, manipulate, or engineer.

Children need the same kind of intoxicating faith that comes when they allow God to do amazing things through their lives. They need a hands-on encounter with ministry that will give them a personal sense of God's mission. They need the passion that results when you collide with crisis to care for someone in a dangerous situation. When there is nothing challenging or adventurous about your style of faith, you begin to drift toward other things that seem more interesting and meaningful. Be honest—what kind of faith experiences are you creating for your children? What stretches their faith? Are you encouraging them to depend on God to do something in them and through them, something they could never possibly do on their own?

Throughout this book, we've been talking about Moses and the speech that he gave to the Israelites just outside Canaan. But there is one thing about this story we haven't said.

The Family Redefined

In the Hebrew culture, systems of faith converged automatically with systems of family. The people that Moses spoke to that day had a belief in God that was central to every custom. It was intertwined seamlessly into routines, celebrations, and feast days. Every leader, parent, priest, prophet, and family operated from the same context of belief and religious practice. In many ways, this kind of collective integrated faith seems ideal.

But the message Moses gave was not intended to be a complete or ideal picture of family life.

Unless we separate the cultural practices of the Israelites from the timeless principles that Moses taught, we will have to sleep in tents, wear robes, eat manna, live like nomads, and practice some pretty strange customs. We are called, however, to learn from the transferable values of Deuteronomy 6 and apply them to our changing culture.

Beyond cultural differences, there is one more significant reason that we have to be careful in the way we apply Deuteronomy 6. Something happened more than a thousand years after Moses that added a new meaning to the role of family. It just so happened that another Jewish leader made a farewell speech. He was also explaining to a group of Hebrew men the importance of transferring faith. Only this leader wasn't merely a prophet or a patriarch. He was God's own Son.

Just before He made a dramatic exit from this planet, Jesus stood on a hillside and told the crowd who had gathered to "go into all the world."[1] He told them to do what He had done. He had entered Hebrew culture as God in the flesh. Now He was urging them to go into foreign cultures to tell His story. He sent them as missionaries into communities where people did not operate from the same context of the Hebrew family.

Why does this matter? We are suggesting that it matters because it illuminates the most fundamental purpose of your family. Because of Jesus, we know that God desires to connect your family and your children to a very specific mission. God doesn't want you to simply keep your faith to yourself. He desires that you understand and connect with different cultures—perhaps *very* different cultures—to translate the story of God's redemptive plan into their language and to present the gospel in new terms.

Jesus changed the rules for every family that follows Him. Even as a Jew, raised in Jewish culture, His goal was not to force people to conform to ancient Jewish family traditions—but to lead all people, from all cultures, to understand God's story. No wonder the apostle Paul said he would be all things to all people.[2] The way that faith and family intersect has to be redefined in light of Jesus' directive to take the church beyond its original context and culture.

If you read Moses' speech only in the context of Deuteronomy, you will understand how the Hebrew family and the Hebrew nation insulated themselves in order to preserve the remnant that would survive against all odds to portray God's love to an outside world. But when you read Moses' speech in light of who Jesus is and what Jesus taught, you understand that now God's people are called to invite others into the spiritual family and to declare God's story to every culture.

Moses spoke to a group of people who represented a subculture that was passive about reaching other cultures, but Jesus has called us to actively influence every society … even to the very ends of the earth.

The principles that Moses taught about loving God and transferring faith still hold true. He represented an Orange way of thinking. He rallied everybody, parents and leaders, to partner for the sake of a generation's future. He understood the potential of family in leveraging a generation to *demonstrate* God's faithfulness.

Many modern models of family and church lean heavily toward creating an insulated protective bubble around each separately. Although it may not be their intent, they seem to be defining something that aligns with the Old Testament practice instead of a New Testament mission. Thousands of years of history took on a different meaning once Jesus started inviting people who were on the outside to participate in His story. All leaders and parents are called to lead their children to *be* the church, not to keep children *in* the church. When we simply protect and preserve, we make the same mistake the one servant made in the parable of the talents. We cover our children with our fear and lack of faith. We hinder their potential to make the kind of difference in the kingdom that they were designed to make.

If you hope to parent beyond your capacity, then you need to connect your children to a mission that is greater than your capacity. Incite their hearts to engage in a purpose bigger than just themselves—and even bigger than just your family. When your children engage in a bigger story, **When your children engage in a bigger story, they are linked to the nature of God's love, which will carry them far beyond what human love will ever have the capacity to do.** they are linked to the nature of God's love, which will carry them far beyond what human love will ever have the capacity to do. *At the heart of every family is a primary calling to lead a generation to the heart of a perfect, loving Father.*

- It is an *authentic* love that connects us to wider circles of a faith community.
- It is an *infinite* love that is links to God's character and faithfulness to our destiny.
- It is a *compelling* love that moves us to trust Him with our hearts, minds, and strength.
- It is an *everyday* love that is developed throughout rhythm of our daily lives.
- It is a *contagious* love that we demonstrate to each other personally.

Our calling as parents is to highlight a divine drama. We have to be intentional in telling children about the ongoing love story between God's people and Himself. We should understand that the primary purpose of the family is to show them God's love through that relationship and invite them to embrace their part in His story. Because when they do:

As a parent, you do have limitations. But that's okay, because there is a really big God and an authentic community waiting to extend capacity far beyond your own.

… they will become a part of a mission-driven community passionate about demonstrating God's love to a broken world.

… they will begin to develop a unique view of the world and life. They will be challenged with a perspective that keeps God as the focus for their personal destiny and direction.

... they will see the potential of God's faithfulness through time and will transition through seasons of their lives growing in their understanding of His love for them.

... they will establish an authentic faith that can grow on a daily basis.

... they will learn the value of demonstrating their personal pursuit of God for the generations that follow after them.

As a parent, you do have limitations. But that's okay, because there is a really big God and an authentic community waiting to extend capacity far beyond your own. If you are like us, your understanding of God has been stretched and shaped by your children. There are probably times they have affected your faith more than you have theirs.

I (Reggie) remember that when my daughter Sarah was four years old, I had been working through some frustrating situations over a period of a several months. Candidly, I was not in a good place emotionally. I left the house to go for a long drive to sort through some issues, and Sarah insisted on going with me. She had the same relational sensitivity then that she has now.

I had been wrestling with a number of important decisions. During the drive I became hyperfocused and preoccupied with thinking through my stuff. It was almost like Sarah was tuned into to the fact that I was stressed, because during the entire two-hour ride she remained completely quiet and still in the passenger's seat. I tried to analyze my situation from every possible angle that day, but it left me feeing kind of hopeless and empty. I'm ashamed to admit that I actually forgot Sarah was in the car.

I pulled into our driveway with everything still unresolved, opened the car door, and began to get out. Then I heard her voice for the first time since we left the house. It was such an interruption to my state of mind that it actually startled me.

"Daddy," she said. "Don't forget me. I have to get out through your door!"

Then I remembered. The door on her side of the car was too heavy for her to open, so we had this routine. I would open my door, and she would crawl out across my lap while I held it. She had said those words to me many times before, but that day it was a striking reminder from God about my relationship with Him. It may have been the first time I understood what it really meant to look at God as my Father.

I walked into the house and went straight back to my bedroom. I closed the door, dropped to my knees, and prayed out loud, "God, I don't think I have understood how You love me as Father. I need You to know that the door on my side is too heavy for me to open. I need You to show up for me today. I need You to open a door that only You can open. I have to get out through Your side."

I had an overwhelming sense of relief and peace when I embraced the reality that God was actively my Father, and He felt the kind of love for me that I felt for Sarah.

We believe that this kind of love is available to every family on the planet. We have seen its ability to transform individuals and restore homes. We know that it has been the primary message God has desired to communicate through time.

It is the reason …

He designed the world.

He created man and woman.

He spoke through Moses.

He made a covenant with a race of people.

He sent His Son to become human.

He died on a cross.

He has promised those who follow Him

they will live forever with Him.

God's love for you and your family has been part of His plan since the beginning of His story. It invites you to a wider community of faith. It is there to remind you of the issues that really matter in life. It gives you the strength you need to fight for your relationships. It is steady, unchanging, and always present. It compels you to personally respond to His message. His love is your best hope to influence your children far beyond the human limits and capacity you have as a parent.

Notes

Chapter 2

1 Deuteronomy 6:4–12.

Chapter 3

1 Meredith Miller, "Family Ministry: Good Things Come in Threes," Fuller Youth Institute, September 5, 2007, http://fulleryouthinstitute.org/2007/09/family-ministry.

2 Deuteronomy 6:2.

3 Mark Kelly, "LifeWay Research: Parents, Churches Can Help Teens Stay in Church," LifeWay Christian Resources, www.lifeway.com/article/?id=165950.

4 Seth Godin, *Tribes: We Need You to Lead Us* (New York: Penguin Portfolio, 2008), 3.

5 Diana Garland, *Inside Out Families: Living the Faith Together* (Waco, TX: Baylor University Press, 2010).

6 Heather Zempel, *Sacred Roads* (Nashville: Threads Media, 2010), 39.

7 Michael Ungar, *We Generation: Raising Socially Responsible Kids* (Toronto: McLelland and Stuart, 2009), 77. While Ungar does not necessarily approach this from an evangelical perspective, he offers strong principles for mentor relationships.

Chapter 4

1 Deuteronomy 6:4.

2 Isadore Singer and Cyrus Adler, eds., *The Jewish Encyclopedia* (New York: Funk & Wagnalls, 1906), 267.

3 The Barna Group, "Parents Accept Responsibility for Their Child's Spiritual Development But Struggle With Effectiveness," *The Barna Update,* May 6, 2003.

4 Hal Runkel, *ScreamFree Parenting* (Duluth, GA: ScreamFree Living, 2005), 70.

Chapter 5

1 Deuteronomy 6:4.

2 Deuteronomy 6:5.

3 Deuteronomy 6:21–24.

4 Chap Clark, *Hurt* (Grand Rapids, MI: Baker Academic, 2004), 110.

5 Richard Halverson, *No Greater Power* (Sisters, OR: Multnomah Press, 1986), 104.

Chapter 6

1 Roy Zuck, ed., *Bibliotheca Sacra* 121 (1965): 228–235.

2 Deuteronomy 6:6–9

3 Matthew 22:35–36.

4 Matthew 22:37.

5 Matthew 22:39–40.

Chapter 7

1 Deuteronomy 6:6.

2 Joyce Martin, et al., "Births: Final Data for 2006," *National Vital Statistics Reports* 57.7 (January 7, 2009), www.cdc.gov/nchs/data/nvsr/nvsr57/nvsr57_07.pdf.

3 Malcolm Gladwell, *Outliers* (New York: Little, Brown and Company, 2008), 40.

4 Madeline Levine, *The Price of Privilege* (New York: HarperCollins, 2006), 204.

5 A number of years ago, Gary Thomas wrote *Sacred Pathways* (Grand Rapids, MI: Zondervan, 1996), a book that highlighted that we are designed to connect with God in different ways. If you are looking to make meaningful spiritual deposits, it's worth a read. North Point Community Church offered a series and self-exam based on this book. Access the exam at http://common.northpoint.org/sacredpathway.html.

6 Gordon MacDonald, *Renewing Your Spiritual Passion* (Nashville, TN: Thomas Nelson, 1997), 71.

Chapter 8

1 Mark 16:15.

2 1 Corinthians 9:22.

About the Authors

Photo by Ken Hawkins

Reggie Joiner is the founder and CEO of the reThink Group, a non-profit organization providing resources and training for parents and churches to maximize their influence on the spiritual growth of the next generation.

The reThink Group provides innovative resources and training for leaders to create relevant, effective environments and strategies for preschoolers, elementary children, families, teenagers, and college students. The reThink Group has partners throughout the United States and eight other countries. The reThink Group is also the architect and primary sponsor of the Orange Conference and the Orange Tour, which provide national training opportunities for senior pastors, church leaders, and ministry volunteers.

Reggie is one of the founding pastors, along with Andy Stanley, of North Point Community Church in Alpharetta, Georgia. In his role as executive director of Family Ministry, Reggie developed groundbreaking concepts of ministry for preschool, children, students, and married adults over the course of his eleven years with the church. During his time with North Point Ministries, Reggie created KidStuf, a weekly environment where kids bring their parents to learn about God, and joined with Andy Stanley, John Maxwell, and Lanny Donoho to create Catalyst, an international conference that attracts more than ten thousand next-generation leaders each year. He has been cohost of Catalyst for the past ten years.

Reggie is the author of *Think Orange: Imagine the Impact When Church and Family Collide*, *Seven Practices of Effective Ministries* (with Andy Stanley and Lane Jones), *Slow Fade*, *The Orange Leaders Handbook,* and a host of other resources. He and his wife, Debbie, live north of Atlanta and have four grown children: Reggie Paul, Hannah, Sarah, and Rebekah.

Photo by Mike Guilbault

Carey Nieuwhof is the lead and founding pastor of Connexus Community Church, a church with campuses in Barrie and Orillia, Ontario, north of Toronto. The vision of Connexus is to create a church that unchurched people love to attend, and its mission is to lead people into a growing relationship with Christ. Connexus is a strategic partner of North Point Ministries and has been Orange from the time it launched in 2007.

Prior to starting Connexus, Carey led three mainline congregations through a decade of transition. He began as a student pastor in 1995. The churches sold their historic buildings and merged to form a new church with a outward-focused mission and in the process, grew from an attendance of 50 in 1995 to over 800 a decade later.

Carey holds degrees in history, law, and theology. In addition to pastoring Connexus, blogging, and writing, Carey often speaks to church leaders across North America about families and leadership. Carey and his wife, Toni, live north of Barrie, Ontario with their sons, Jordan and Sam.

**ORANGE IS A UNIQUE STRATEGY FOR
COMBINING THE CRITICAL INFLUENCES
IN LIFE TO FUEL FAITH IN THE NEXT
GENERATION**

IT'S A STRATEGY THAT SYNCHRONIZES THE INFLUENCE OF PARENTS AND CHURCH LEADERS TOWARD A COMPREHENSIVE PLAN FROM PRESCHOOL TO COLLEGE

FIRST LOOK PRESCHOOL CURRICULUM
252 BASICS CHILDREN'S CURRICULUM
XP3 STUDENT CURRICULUM

THINK ORANGE PUBLISHED MATERIALS
ORANGE LEADERS TRAINING RESOURCES
ORANGE CONFERENCE & TOUR
ORANGE PARENTS RESOURCES

CAMP KIDJAM
AMBER SKY MUSIC

www.OrangeThinkers.com

www.Studio252.tv
A website for kids.

Videos, games, blogs, Bible stories, music, artwork